KILLER B's

The Boston Bruins Capture Their First Stanley Cup in 39 Years

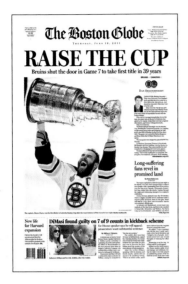

RAISE THE CUP

Bruins shut the door in Game 7 to take first title in 39 years

Long-suffering fans revel in promised land

New life for Harvard expansion

DiMasi found guilty on 7 of 9 counts in kickback scheme

Stanley Cup champions

Glory B's!

Bruins vanquish Canucks for sixth championship in franchise history

The Boston Globe

Triumph Books and colophon are registered trademarks of Random House, Inc.

This book is available in quantity at special discounts for your group or organization. For further information, contact:

Triumph Books
542 South Dearborn Street
Suite 750
Chicago, Illinois 60605
(312) 939-3330
Fax (312) 663-3557
www.triumphbooks.com

Printed in U.S.A.
ISBN: 978-1-60078-683-9

TRIUMPH
BOOKS

BOOK STAFF
EDITOR Janice Page
ART DIRECTOR Rena Anderson Sokolow
DESIGNERS Cindy Daniels, Jerome Layman Jr.
ASSISTANT EDITOR Ron Driscoll
WRITERS/RESEARCHERS Mark Cofman, Rob Duca

PHOTOGRAPHERS
THE BOSTON GLOBE John Blanding, 117
• Yoon S. Byun, 11, 68, 95, 108 • Charles Carey, 115
• Barry Chin, 18-19, 23, 28, 35-37, 50-51, 58-59, 61-65, 97, 104 • Jim Davis, front cover, 7, 12-15, 26, 29-31, 40-43, 46, 78, 80-81, 84- 87, 89, 94, 105, 128 • Evan Richman, 117 • Stan Grossfeld, 87 • Suzanne Kreiter, 5, 106 • Matthew J. Lee, 52 • Frank O'Brien, 112-114, 117-119 • John Tlumacki, 14, 16, 18, 22, 24, 38, 44-45, 52, 66, 67, 73-77, 82-83, 89, 93, 96, 103-106, 116, 120, back cover.

ADDITIONAL PHOTOS COURTESY OF
AP/Wide World Photos, 20 (Julie Jacobson), 89 (Charles Krupa), 94 (Katerina Sulova), 98 (Sean Kilpatrick), 100 (Kathy Kmonicek, John Ulan), 110, 111; Aram Boghosian, 52 • Elsa/Getty Images, 48, 57-58 (Bruce Bennett), 89 (Eliot J. Schechter, Harry How), 100 (Dave Sandford), 110 (Bruce Bennett) • Reuters, 12 (Mike Blake), 99 (Ben Nelms), 101 (Blair Gable), 102 (Shaun Best), 126 (Ben Nelms); UPI, 69, 115.

With special thanks to Joe Sullivan and the Boston Globe sports department; Jim Wilson, Susan Vermazen, Cecille Avila, and the Boston Globe photo department; Jerry Melvin; Lisa Tuite and the Boston Globe library staff.

Front cover Tim Thomas got some well-earned minutes with the NHL's most coveted trophy.
Opposite page The Paul Revere statue in Boston's North End was outfitted for the finals, perhaps to warn of new foes from British Columbia?
Back cover Bruins fans showed their colors as they passed the team banner at TD Garden.

CONTENTS

FOR NEARLY FOUR DECADES THEY'D BEEN AN ALSO-RAN in a city of champions. Since the Bruins last had their paws on Lord Stanley's mug in 1972 the Celtics had won six NBA titles, the Patriots three Super Bowls, and the Red Sox two World Series. This, finally, was the year when Boston became a hockey town again, when the Garden floor remained frozen until the middle of June, when Tank and Looch and Marshy and Bergy and Z and their spoked-B brethren growled and clawed their way to a most unlikely championship during an endless winter.

NO BUNCH OF BRUINS EVER WORKED LONGER or journeyed farther for glory than did this one, playing 25 games and traveling the equivalent of more than halfway around the planet before hoisting the trophy inside a hostile building in Vancouver, where Claude Julien's bearded workingmen played the game

I N T R O

of their lives when it mattered most. No NHL club ever had won three seventh games on the way to the Cup and no Boston team ever had lost the first two games of a playoff series and survived. This one did it twice.

THE BRUINS WERE DEAD MEN SKATING after going down 0-2 to the Canadiens on Causeway Street. But Tim Thomas, the masked man who hadn't played a minute during last year's post-season but was this year's MVP, revived his mates in Montreal and Nathan Horton clinched the series in overtime of the seventh game on his only shot.

ONLY ONE ENCOUNTER WAS EASY, a sweep of Philadelphia that expunged the bitter memory of last season's epic collapse. The Tampa Bay series came down to the 52d minute of the seventh game and one goal, again by Horton.

AND AFTER THE BRUINS DROPPED THE FIRST TWO meetings in Vancouver, they battered the Canucks three times in the Garden, then finished them off by a 4-0 count in their own building.

THEY WERE BORN IN QUEBEC, Slovakia, Germany, Finland, Czech Republic, and Michigan. but these Bruins lived by the same "all-for-one" watch word as did Bobby and Espo and Turk and Pie and Cheesy and Chief 39 years ago. This time, it was their party and their parade.⊛

Claude Julien got the last laugh.

798

Tim Thomas set records for the most saves in a single postseason (798) and in a Stanley Cup finals (238).

43

Mark Recchi retires at 43 with the fourth-most games played in NHL history (1,652) and is 12th all-time in points scored (1,533). He is also the only player on the Bruins roster who was alive in 1972, when Boston last won the Cup.

16

Bruins' captain Zdeno Chara led the playoff rankings with a plus/minus of 16.

11

Brad Marchand scored 11 goals in the playoffs to tie Jeremy Roenick (Chicago, 1990) for the second-most ever by a rookie.

2

The Canucks' Ryan Kesler, Henrik Sedin, and Daniel Sedin, who combined for 101 goals in the regular season, combined for two goals in the finals against the Bruins.

The Bruins decided that the script for this Stanley Cup drama was getting a bit formulaic: close, gnawing defeats in the Pacific Northwest followed by dominating victories at home. So they rewrote the ending and joined the Cup legacies of Schmidt, Shore, and Orr.

CANUCKS BRUINS

Game 1

1-0

BOS	0	0	0		0
VAN	0	0	1		1

WEDNESDAY, JUNE 1, 2011 • **VANCOUVER**

Game 2

3-2

BOS	0	2	0	0	2
VAN	1	0	1	1	3

SATURDAY, JUNE 4, 2011 • **VANCOUVER**

Game 3

8-1

VAN	0	0	1		1
BOS	0	4	4		8

MONDAY, JUNE 6, 2011 • **BOSTON**

Game 4

4-0

VAN	0	0	0		0
BOS	1	2	1		4

WEDNESDAY, JUNE 8, 2011 • **BOSTON**

Game 5

1-0

BOS	0	0	0		0
VAN	0	0	1		1

FRIDAY, JUNE 10, 2011 • **VANCOUVER**

Game 6

5-2

VAN	0	0	2		2
BOS	4	0	1		5

MONDAY, JUNE 13, 2011 • **BOSTON**

Game 7

4-0

BOS	1	2	1		4
VAN	0	0	0		0

WEDNESDAY, JUNE 15, 2011 • **VANCOUVER**

DESTINY

VERSUS
VAN COUVER

THEY WON IT FOR EVERY NEW ENGLAND MOM AND DAD who ever woke up to drive kids to the rink at 6 a.m., and drank hot chocolate while they waited in the cold. They won it for the Revere girls with the big hair and O'Reilly sweaters; for the shot-and-beer guys who pour every dollar of expendable income into the hockey budget. They won it to avenge losing Bobby Orr to Chicago, too many men on the ice in Montreal, free agents never signed, trades that went bad, unspeakable injuries, and Game 7 disappointments. They won it for you.

THE BOSTON BRUINS WON THE STANLEY CUP, shocking the Vancouver Canucks, 4-0, capping an epic seven-game series and bringing the holy grail to the Hub of Hockey for the first time since 1972. The goals were

THE CUP

scored by Patrice Bergeron and Brad (Little Ball Of Hate) Marchand, two apiece. The non-goals were stopped by playoff MVP Tim Thomas.

AT THIS HOUR, EVERYMAN THOMAS IS TOM BRADY, Bill Russell, and Curt Schilling. And the Bruins are Stanley Cup champs. They outscored the favored Canucks by a whopping 23-8 over seven games. Thomas addressed Cup-starved Boston fans, saying, "You've been waiting for it a long time, but you got it. You wanted it, you got it. We're bringing it home."

"IT'S SURREAL," SAID MARCHAND. "I don't know if it will ever kick in." Marchand is a rookie. He is from Hammond Plains, Nova Scotia. He is 23 years old. How could he possibly know what this moment is like for longtime Bruins fans? How could any of the champion Bruins know?

"IT'S UNREAL," SAID CLUB PRESIDENT CAM NEELY, a man who skated and suffered through some of the tough years. "You dream about a moment like this and you don't know how you're gonna feel. I'm so proud of the whole group."

"I GUESS THERE IS A SANTA CLAUS," said Jeremy Jacobs, who has › PAGE 17

A Bruins' fan hoped the Black and Gold would draw Game 4 inspiration from the loss of Nathan Horton and Marc Savard to season-ending concussions.

G A M E 1

Both teams served notice that this would be a highly physical Stanley Cup finals, but the Bruins felt Canucks' forward Alex Burrows (above) stepped over the line when he appeared to bite Patrice Bergeron's finger during a scrum behind the Boston net at the end of the first period. Bergeron (right) pointed out the evidence after the altercation, which resulted in a double-minor penalty to Burrows for roughing. Adding insult to injury, the Bruins lost the opener, 1-0.

1-0

GAME 2

The heavy hitting continued at Rogers Arena in Game 2, including this bone-crunching first-period collision (right) between the Bruins' Dennis Seidenberg and Vancouver's Victor Oreskovich. Nothing was more painful to the Bruins than the sight of the puck sliding into an empty goal (below) courtesy of the Canucks' Alex Burrows, who dodged a suspension for his Game 1 antics and scored 11 seconds into overtime when he swept behind the net ahead of defenseman Zdeno Chara and deftly potted the winner.

GAME 3

The NHL's crackdown this season on blindside hits and blows to the head became the focal point of Game 3 in Boston after Canucks' defenseman Aaron Rome delivered a violent first-period hit (far left) to the Bruins' Nathan Horton. Horton, who had already passed the puck when he was leveled, was left flat on his back and was taken to Massachusetts General Hospital. The Bruins won the game, 8-1, but lost Horton (concussion) for the remainder of the series. Rome, who drew a five-minute interference major and game misconduct on the play, was suspended for four games, ending his postseason as well.

Defenseman Andrew Alberts and the rest of the Canucks were helpless to stop the barrage of Bruins' goals that followed Nathan Horton's injury. Alberts, a Boston College product and former Bruin, had to look away as his ex-teammates celebrated Mark Recchi's third-period goal. The game was scoreless when Horton was carried off the ice at 5:07 of the first period, and though they failed to capitalize on their five-minute power play, the Bruins scored four unanswered goals in the second period and found the back of the net four more times in the third for a runaway victory that cut their series deficit to 2-1.

FROM 10 •
owned the Bruins since 1975 and earned a reputation as the Montgomery Burns of Boston sports.

No more. It's all good now. The kind folks inside Rogers Arena in Vancouver let the Bruins hang around the ice with the Cup for almost an hour after the game and played "Dirty Water" and "Tessie" over the public address system as Boston players embraced their families and friends and posed with the Cup.

Too bad they didn't play "We Are The Champions."

Today would be a good day to call your out-of-town friends and tell them you live in a city that just won its seventh championship in 11 years.

You live in the only hamlet that's won the Grand Slam of North American trophies within seven years.

It is the High Renaissance of New England sports. Our Duck Boat tires are balding. The vaunted Patriots just became the Boston franchise with the longest championship drought. The Patriots, the NFL's team of the decade, haven't won a Super Bowl since way back in 2005.

The humanity!

Let the record show that the Bruins' long-awaited return to the circle of champions came on a perfect June evening, 2,500 miles across the continent from Causeway Street. A season that started in Prague ended on Game No. 107, as the Bruins became the first team in NHL history to win three Game 7s in a single spring. It was the Bruins' first Game 7 road win in their 87-year history. And it was stunning.

A seven-game series that had finger-biting, taunting, trash talk, and embellishment ended with Bruin dominance. After losing three one-goal games at Rogers Arena, the Bruins took the fight out of the locals in the finale. Vancouver's only fight was demonstrated by nitwits who rioted after the game — fires raged and tear gas was released, giving the city another black eye.

The Bruins were inspired by the presence of Nathan Horton, who scored the game-winner in both of Boston's first two Game 7s, then was felled by Aaron Rome's late hit in Game 3 of the Stanley Cup finals. Horton splashed some Boston water on the Vancouver ice for good luck long before the start of last night's game.

"This is the chance of a lifetime to be with my teammates," he said afterward. "I couldn't miss this."

The Canucks were strong at the jump, but with 5 1/2 minutes left in the first period, the Bruins lost a faceoff in the Vancouver zone, but Marchand got the puck. The Ball Of Hate controlled it nicely, and centered the puck to Bergeron, who one-timed it past Roberto Luongo. Good omen. The team that scored first won every game of the Final.

Late in the second, Zdeno Chara made a crucial save. That's right. Save. After giving up the puck right in front of the Bruins' net, he assumed the goalie duties when Thomas was faked out of position.

Looking like a treetop Gump Worsley, Chara stopped Alex Burrows's shot with his left knee. Nice save for the big guy.

With 7:47 left in the second, Marchand made it 2-0 on a wraparound at the left post. Once again, tire-pumpin' Luongo was not agile enough to stop the puck.

Then the Bruins struck with a shorthanded goal — the clincher. With Chara off for interference (first penalty of the night), Bergeron found himself on a shorthanded partial breakaway. As he was dragged down by Christian Ehrhoff (chasing with Alex Edler), Bergeron somehow steered the puck past the shell-shocked Luongo. The goal was reviewed and when it was announced that the goal would count, it sounded like 18,860 were taking their college boards. The Bruins had three goals on only 13 shots. Both Sedins were on the ice for all three scores. At that juncture, Luongo had whiffed on six of the last 21 shots on net.

Back in Boston, the countdown was underway. Marchand potted an empty-netter with 2:44 left. Claude Julien made sure Mark Recchi was on the ice at the end.

To the finish, Thomas remained in full Battlefly, wielding his Reebok war club like Russell Crowe in "Gladiator." Kevin Bieksa fired the puck the length of the ice as the whistle sounded. Perfect. Thomas had the puck and the Bruins had the Cup.

As for the other goalie? Here's the new joke in British Columbia:

Q: What time is it in Vancouver?

A: It's 20 past Luongo.

Actually, it was party time for the Boston contingent on the Rogers Arena ice.

At 10:52 (Boston time), the Cup appeared and NHL commissioner Gary Bettman beckoned Chara. The captain skated toward the commissioner, hoisted the chalice, skated in a circle, then presented it to 43-year-old Recchi.

Recchi had just played his last game. The veteran forward took his turn, then passed the Cup to Bergeron, who relayed it to Thomas. On and on it went. They're probably still passing it to one another as you read this. ⊚

G A M E 4

Game 4 at TD Garden was a tale of two goalies. A frustrated Roberto Luongo (above) was pulled from the game after allowing Rich Peverley's third-period goal (left) to close the scoring in the Bruins' 4-0 victory, while Tim Thomas (right) made his triumphant exit at game's end with a magnificent 38-save shutout. The Bruins and Canucks were even at two games apiece and headed back to Vancouver.

4-0

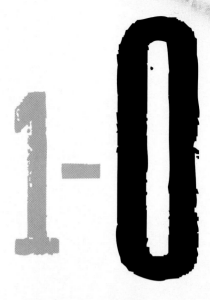

1-0

G A M E 5

The Bruins had exploded for 12 goals in their two victories in Boston, but drew blanks in Vancouver while Maxim Lapierre managed to beat goalie Tim Thomas at 4:35 of the third period with the lone tally of Game 5. Despite being outscored, 12-1, in their two series losses, the Canucks' dramatic victory gave them a 3-2 series lead, with all three of their wins secured at Rogers Arena by one-goal margins.

The Bruins continued to make life in Boston miserable for Vancouver goalie Roberto Luongo, who was removed from Game 6 after allowing three goals on the first eight shots. Luongo, who was also replaced in Game 3 at TD Garden, yielded goals (left deck, top to bottom) to Brad Marchand, Milan Lucic, and Andrew Ference before backup Cory Schneider was beaten by Michael Ryder for the Bruins' fourth goal of the period, setting a record for fastest four goals in finals history. In a familiar series scene (right), things got testy in the third period with the Canucks' Kevin Bieksa getting the worst of this scrum.

5-2

GAME 6

Working with an early four-goal cushion, Bruins' goalie Tim Thomas was his usual brilliant self, denying the Canucks a chance to climb back into the contest. Thomas made 36 stops, including this second-period gem off the stick of Vancouver winger Victor Oreskovich.

4-0

G A M E 7

Patrice Bergeron (37) was a picture of joy celebrating his first-period goal with teammates Brad Marchand and Mark Recchi. Bergeron's goal opened the Game 7 scoring at 14:37, and he added a shorthanded goal in the second period to give the Bruins a commanding 3-0 lead. Bergeron's performance capped a stellar individual postseason, which was very much in doubt some five weeks earlier when he suffered a concussion in the Eastern Conference semifinals against Philadelphia.

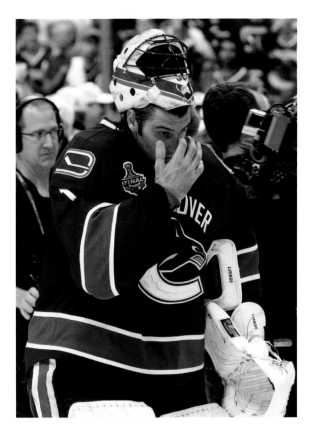

G A M E 7

The list of Canucks who turned in disappointing performances in the series was lengthy, but Roberto Luongo's name fell squarely at the top. Luongo, who was roughed up early and often in the Bruins' three victories in Boston, could do little to stem the tide in Game 7 at Rogers Arena. He was subjected to the sight of Brad Marchand's victory leap (right) into the waiting arms of Zdeno Chara following his second-period goal to give the Bruins a 2-0 lead. Marchand added a third-period empty-netter for good measure moments before Luongo made his painful exit from the ice (above) at game's end.

G A M E 7

Nathan Horton (above), such an integral part of the Bruins' magical postseason march before a concussion ended his season in Game 3 of the Stanley Cup finals, was all smiles as he joined teammates Adam McQuaid (54) and Tyler Seguin for a post-game celebration. Tim Thomas (right) gave Patrice Bergeron a king-sized victory hug after posting his second shutout of the series to cap a brilliant postseason that earned him the Conn Smythe Trophy as playoff MVP. Thomas allowed the high-powered Canucks' offense just eight goals in seven games, stopping all 37 shots in the grand finale.

The Bruins played some ragged hockey, and no lead seemed safe with St. Louis & Company buzzing. But they saved their backchecking best for last with a complete team effort in a 1-0 Game 7 classic.

LIGHTNING BRUINS

Game 1

5-2

TB	3	0	2	5
BOS	1	0	1	2

SATURDAY, MAY 14, 2011 • **BOSTON**

Game 2

6-5

TB	2	1	2	5
BOS	1	5	0	6

TUESDAY, MAY 17, 2011 • **BOSTON**

Game 3

2-0

BOS	1	0	1	2
TB	0	0	0	0

THURSDAY, MAY 19, 2011 • **TAMPA BAY**

Game 4

5-3

BOS	3	0	0	3
TB	0	3	2	5

SATURDAY, MAY 21, 2011 • **TAMPA BAY**

Game 5

3-1

TB	1	0	0	1
BOS	0	2	1	3

MONDAY, MAY 23, 2011 • **BOSTON**

Game 6

5-4

BOS	2	0	2	4
TB	1	2	2	5

WEDNESDAY, MAY 25, 2011 • **TAMPA BAY**

Game 7

1-0

TB	0	0	0	0
BOS	0	0	1	1

FRIDAY, MAY 27, 2011 • **BOSTON**

ELECTRICITY

SIXTY MINUTES. ONE GOAL. THAT'S ALL TIM THOMAS NEEDED. It was 60 minutes of clean, breathtaking, exquisite hockey in the most important game of the year. It was a Game 7 for the ages, and with their 1-0 victory over the Tampa Bay Lightning, the Boston Bruins advanced to the Stanley Cup finals for the first time since 1990.

THE LIGHTNING MADE THE BRUINS WORK FOR THIS WIN until the final seconds. How closely matched were these teams, who each had finished with 103 points during the regular season? Well, they each scored 21 goals in this series. Does that tell you anything? "We had nothing left," said

R O U N D 3

Tampa Bay coach Guy Boucher. "Nothing left in the tank." There was a certain irony in this outcome, since this was the second 1-0 Game 7 in which the Lightning were involved this year. That's the score by which they completed a comeback from a 3-1 first-round series deficit against the Pittsburgh Penguins.

THIS ONE TURNED BOSTON'S WAY when Nathan Horton took a left-to-right feed from David Krejci and slipped it into the net at 12:27 of the third period, thus setting off an agonizing finish during which the delirious sellout crowd of 17,565 made more and more noise until the final horn. I don't think I've ever heard this second version of the Boston Garden rock to this extent. Some in attendance have been waiting a very long time for something this good to happen involving their beloved Boston Bruins. Few have been treated to a better game of hockey.

THERE'S NOTHING IN SPORT QUITE LIKE STANLEY CUP HOCKEY, especially Stanley Cup overtime, when one teeny-weeny mistake can lead to disaster and the end of a season. Wait, this wasn't overtime? Tell it to the principals. "It felt like overtime the whole game," Boucher confessed. This was not just a game of clean, breathtaking, exquisite hockey. It was a game of clean, breathtaking, exquisite, and penalty-free hockey. That's correct. Neither referee Dan O'Halloran nor referee › PAGE 37

Nathan Horton (left) and Tim Thomas, heroes in the first two rounds of the playoffs, did it again in Game 7 against Tampa.

The conference finals didn't get off to a good start for the Bruins. Tim Thomas was under siege for much of the game, including this first-period goal by Brett Clark (not pictured) that gave Tampa Bay's Teddy Purcell and Nate Thompson reason to celebrate. At the other end, goalie Dwayne Roloson (right) was the true backbone of the Lightning's solid defensive effort, stopping 31 shots in a 5-2 victory at TD Garden.

5-2

FROM 34 · Stephen Walkom saw the need to raise his right hand to signify an infraction. That's because no player wished to be the guy whose borderline tripping, slashing, boarding, interference, holding the stick, or any other kind of penalty would lead to a damaging power play. If this meant there was less hitting than one might expect, so be it.

Roughing? Are you mad? Not in this game.

"It was a credit to both teams' discipline and attention to detail," Boucher said.

"I think the referees tonight let the two teams decide the outcome," declared Bruins mentor Claude Julien. "I thought the referees handled themselves extremely well."

Now about that Thomas fellow. He was good to very good on a night when he was not called upon to be great. If any goaltender deserved a first star, it would have been Tampa Bay's Dwayne Roloson, who faced many more quality shots than

Thomas. The Bruins took the play to the visitors pretty much from the outset, outshooting Tampa Bay by a 2-1 margin through the first 24 minutes (18-9) and finishing with a 38-24 advantage.

But a combination of Roloson's excellence and the Bruins' inability to finish kept the game scoreless more than 12 minutes into the third period, until Andrew Ference sprung Krejci along the left boards. Krejci deftly slid the puck to Horton, a professional goal scorer who had stationed himself where a goal scorer ought to be. The pass was perfect and the finish was perfunctory. Horton gets the goal and more of the glory, but this play was approximately 80 percent pass and 20 percent finish.

What's significant in all this is that it was the first line that got the job done. There have been times in these playoffs when Milan Lucic, Krejci, and Horton have been criticized for pulling a long-term disappearing act. So give Messrs. Horton and Krejci the requisite props for producing the biggest goal of the year.

Who would have envisioned a trip to the Stanley Cup finals when the Bruins dropped the first two games of the first-round series with Montreal? But they have talked themselves up as a "resilient" team, and now they have walked the walk, winning four of the last five from the Canadiens, sweeping Philadelphia, and then winning the two games they needed in this series after suffering an

embarrassing loss in Game 4, when they were unable to hold a 3-0 lead.

They proved to their fans that they are a far different and better team than the one that lost the final four games of last year's Philadelphia series, led by a 37-year-old goaltender who had lost his job to Tuukka Rask at this time last year. Remember the moaning about Tim Thomas being an overpaid backup? I'm sure he does.

The Bruins knew Thomas would come up as big as he needed to in Game 7 against the Lightning, but they also knew it would be a lot easier on him if they avoided silly turnovers. If Tampa Bay had an odd-man rush, I can't recall it.

And they were never better than in the final seven minutes. "They played great," said Tampa Bay's Vincent Lecavalier. "Once they went up, 1-0, they really came back with those five guys, and it was tough to get anything. We got a few shots, but it was tough to get those rebounds. They really came back, tight, and as a team."

The Bruins were so persistent, the Lightning could barely get Roloson off the ice to get the sixth attacker involved. His first move to the bench with 45 seconds left lasted a second, due to a faceoff. When he was finally able to leave for good, there were only 30.2 seconds left, and it was too late to make a difference.

Sixty minutes. One goal. Now that's a proper Game 7. ⊕

6-5

Youth was served when the Bruins unleashed the offensive skills of Tyler Seguin en route to a series-tying victory. After 11 healthy postseason scratches and just 10 minutes of playing time in the opener, the Bruins' rookie exploded for two goals and two assists in the second period, including the game-tying goal 48 seconds after the puck was dropped. The Bruins finished the period ahead, 6-3, but had to hang on for dear life.

REBELLION

G A M E 3

2-0

Dwayne Roloson had that helpless appearance as he and defenseman Mike Lundin watched Andrew Ference's third-period shot slowly slide past the goal line with Chris Kelly on the doorstep. Kelly and his teammates celebrated the goal, which gave the Bruins insurance en route to a 2-0 victory in Tampa.

David Krejci also scored for the Bruins, while Tim Thomas made 31 stops to record the shutout. It was the first game back for Patrice Bergeron, who suffered a concussion in Game 4 of the previous series.

5-3

GAME 4

The Lightning saluted the St. Pete Times Forum fans following their 5-3 victory in Game 4, which evened the series. Tampa Bay goalie Dwayne Roloson was roughed up for three first-period goals, but was one of the first to congratulate backup Mike Smith, who shut the door on the Bruins thereafter while his teammates scored five unanswered goals. Tampa Bay's stunning comeback began at 6:55 of the second period (below) when Teddy Purcell got the first of his two goals past Tim Thomas, assisted by Simon Gagne (12) with Ryan Malone (6) stationed at the post in case of a rebound.

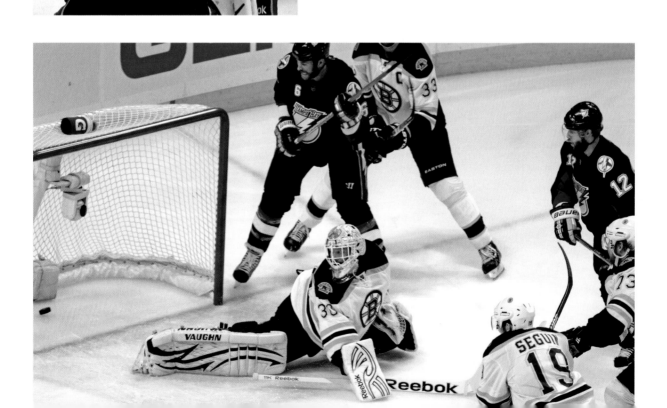

3-1

Reebok

GAME 5

Stick save and a beauty! The stick of goalie Tim Thomas (above) was all that separated a shot by Steve Downie from tying the game in the third period. The game was as physical as it was dramatic, with Tampa Bay's Eric Brewer (left) delivering a hit that sent Patrice Bergeron to the ice, and a scrum of players after time ran out (bottom right).

Brad Marchand's second-period goal had broken a 1-1 tie, and Rich Peverley's empty-netter put the finishing touches on the victory, which gave the Bruins a 3-2 series lead.

5-4

GAME 6

The Bruins were on the wrong end of both the scoreboard and a massive shower of noisemakers tossed from the crowd onto the St. Pete Times Forum ice following the Lightning's 5-4 victory in Game 6. Teddy Purcell and Martin St. Louis each scored a pair of goals for Tampa Bay to offset a hat trick by the Bruins' red-hot David Krejci, that gave him 10 goals for the postseason. A return trip to Boston for Game 7 was next up on the itinerary for the evenly matched Eastern Conference finalists.

GAME 7

Nathan Horton came up as big as ever at 12:27 of the third period, firing the puck past Dwayne Roloson to give the Bruins a 1-0 lead. It was the only goal of Game 7, and would not have been nearly enough to send the Bruins to their first Stanley Cup finals in 21 years if not for the supreme efforts of Tim Thomas, who stopped 24 Tampa Bay shots to record his second shutout of the series.

G A M E 7

1-0

Tim Thomas was congratulated by his current teammates and by a former teammate at the University of Vermont, Tampa's Martin St. Louis, after the Bruins won the Eastern Conference title.

THE FANS DEEP ROOTS KEPT US ROOTING

The Old Guy was patient. The Old Guy knew you'd come around.

Yup, Old Man Hockey knew that deep down in your heart, lodged in the depth of your psyche, there resided a little round rubber disk, right next to that little white ball with the red stitches. Football and basketball have had their moments of glory during the past two decades, but Old Man Hockey knew that the two sports permanently embedded in the local DNA were baseball and, yes, hockey.

Old Man Hockey watched in sadness as other sports elbowed him to the side. But he had faith. He knew you just needed an excuse to reacquaint yourself with a sport that has extremely deep roots in these here parts.

And you have. It has been 21 years since the Boston Bruins have even played for the Cup, and it has been 39 years since they actually won it. So much has changed, on and off the ice. Bobby Orr and Phil Esposito are in their 60s. Even Ray Bourque has hit 50.

There was no music blaring in the Old Garden, and not much in the way of video, either. There was just John Kiley, bringing the Bruins out to "Paree" and rousing the crowd during languid moments with such tunes as "Mexican Hat Dance."

When Johnny "Chief" Bucyk skated around the Garden with Lord Stanley's Cup held aloft following that 1970 triumph, there may have been six people sporting Bruins garb. This time, at least 75 percent of the playoff crowds breaking every decibel record in the newer building were wearing something black and gold, none of it cheap. Being a fan now calls for a far more substantial financial commitment than it did in Ye Olden Days. And we're not even talking about the price of tickets.

The teams are surely different. The last Bruins team to win a Stanley Cup was led by a pair of extraordinary all-time talents who played a far different game. Phil Esposito led the league with 133 points (which sounded good until Wayne Gretzky came along). The incomparable

Bobby Orr augmented his annual Norris Trophy with 117 points. The Chief, who played the regular season at a spry 36, had 83. Six other Bruins had more than 50 points.

That kind of firepower doesn't exist anymore, anywhere. Milan Lucic was this team's only 30-goal scorer, sharing the team scoring lead at a rather modest 62 points with David Krejci. Patrice Bergeron had 57 points. Nathan Horton had 53. So much for 50-point men.

But these guys know how to D-up, as we say in basketball. The Bruins led the Eastern Conference in fewest goals allowed with 195, and that's the way coach Claude Julien likes it. The 1-0 Game 7 conquest of Tampa Bay represented Julien hockey at its finest. The top-to-bottom attention to detail was extraordinary. There were no sloppy passes, no careless puckhandling, and no letdown in forechecking.

The last Bruins team to win a Stanley Cup was easy enough to like, consisting, as it did, of so many A students. But this bunch is lovable more for its collective strength and its downright vulnerability than for its stars.

Well, yes, there is a star aside from Thomas. It's hard not to notice Zdeno Chara. The 6-foot-9-inch Slovakian plays about 7-4 when you throw in his skates and his stick, which enables him to execute poke checks when the play has emanated from Downtown Crossing.

It is a team with little margin for error, and it arrived in the Cup finals with a large stain on its résumé. Most teams love power plays. Some thrive on them. The Bruins would be better off if they could adopt a football policy and refuse penalties.

But Bruins fans have learned to love

them despite their flaws because the game they are playing is hockey and certain elements remain constant, especially in the Stanley Cup playoffs. Your father loved hockey, and so did his father, and maybe even his father.

Detroit fancies itself "Hockeytown"? What a laugh. There is only one "Hockeytown" in America, one town where the NHL has been going on since 1924, one town where high school hockey has an eight-decade tradition, one town where you can stage an annual college hockey tournament featuring four high-quality teams within a 2-mile radius.

The Bruins are right in the center of this hockey consciousness, and have been since the '20s. The first great NHL superstar was Eddie Shore, and guess where he played all those years? We had the great "Kraut Line," champs just before WWII, and, of course, we had the Big Bad Bruins. We had Ray Bourque and Cam Neely.

Granted, it has been a frustrating 21 years for Bruins devotees. There has been a lot of teasing, and little fulfillment, since the 1992 team advanced to the conference finals, only to be slapped around by the mighty Penguins. Only a year ago, the Bruins suffered the most humiliating series loss in NHL history.

But you knew there was something good going on when this team pulled off a 6-0 road trip from February 17 through March 1. That told you this team had an inner resolve other recent Bruins teams lacked. They showed that resolve again after losing Games 1 and 2 at home to Montreal. And here they are, playing the game you and your forefathers have always loved with spunk and heart.

Old Man Hockey knew you'd come around. All you needed was a reason to care. ☺

DETROIT FANCIES ITSELF "HOCKEYTOWN"? WHAT A LAUGH.

The Bruins had waited a year for the chance to redeem themselves and their fans, and they never gave the flummoxed Flyers hope for a single victory – never mind another historic comeback – in their return engagement.

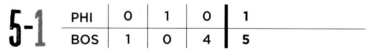

Game 1

7-3

BOS	2	3	2	7
PHI	1	1	1	3

SATURDAY, APRIL 30, 2011 • **PHILADELPHIA**

Game 2

3-2

BOS	2	0	0	1	3
PHI	2	0	0	0	2

MONDAY, MAY 2, 2011 • **PHILADELPHIA**

Game 3

5-1

PHI	0	1	0	1
BOS	2	2	1	5

WEDNESDAY, MAY 4, 2011 • **BOSTON**

Game 4

5-1

PHI	0	1	0	1
BOS	1	0	4	5

FRIDAY, MAY 6, 2011 • **BOSTON**

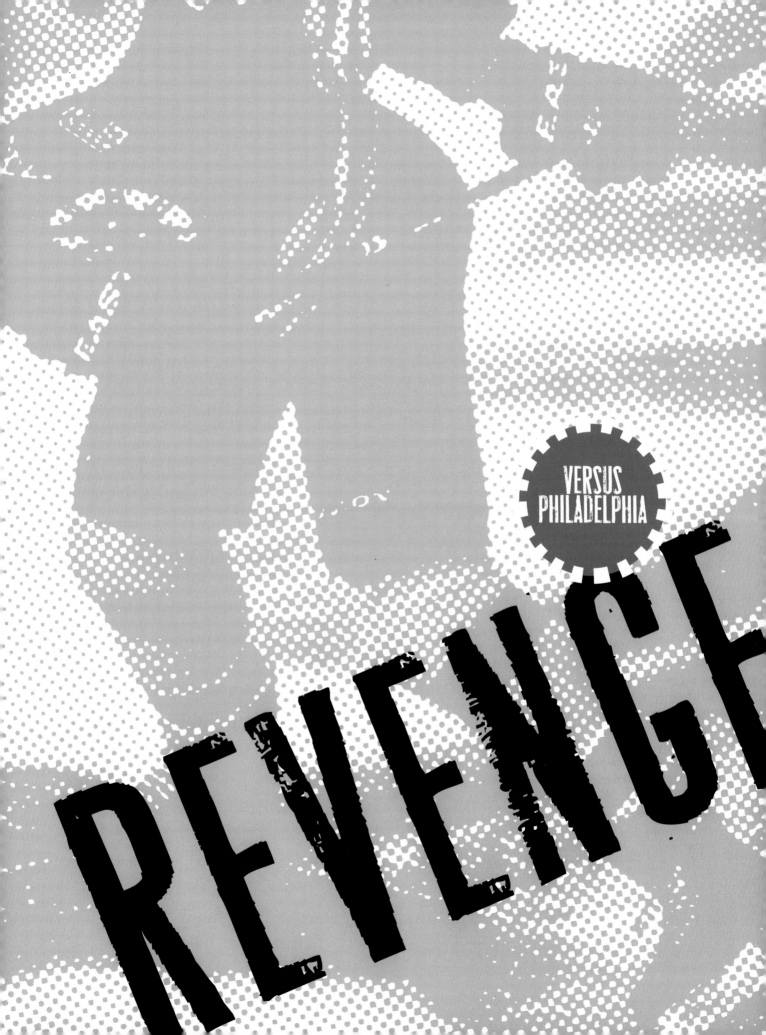

VERSUS
PHILADELPHIA

REVENGE

ROUND 2 IS OVER.

With a convincing 5-1 triumph before 17,565 enraptured followers at TD Garden, the Bruins swept the Philadelphia Flyers out of the NHL playoffs.

REVENGE IS THEIRS. RETRIBUTION IS THEIRS. PEACE OF MIND IS THEIRS.

A year ago, the Bruins suffered the most humiliating loss in their history, blowing a 3-0 series lead and a 3-0 lead in Game 7 at home to the Flyers. One year later, they have crushed the Flyers, outscoring them by a hefty 20-7 margin. This would seem to balance the scales, would it not?

"I HOPE SO," said Boston goaltender Tim Thomas, the team's unquestioned most valuable player in the first two rounds of the playoffs. "You keep hearing about last year, and you have to ignore it to be able to do what we just did, winning this series. But to be honest, I'm glad it's over

R O U N D 2

... because the longer that series would have went, the more talk about last year. So, I'm glad that it is put behind us as a team, and organization, and the fans. I'm glad the fans can put it behind them, too. And I'll say it, hopefully exorcising some demons."

THE BRUINS MADE THE FANS SWEAT A BIT, entering the third period tied at 1-1 after a Brad Marchand giveaway had led to Kris Versteeg's tying goal at 13:22 of the second period. But the third period belonged to the home team, starting with a Johnny Boychuk blast past Flyers goalie Sergei Bobrovsky at 2:42 and ending with Daniel Paille's empty-net tap-in at 19:35, at which point the unofficial Boston sports anthem, "I'm Shipping Up to Boston," had been playing ceaselessly over the PA system for about three minutes.

THE PLAYOFFS HAD BEGUN ON A VERY NEGATIVE NOTE when the Bruins dropped Games 1 and 2 at home to the hated Montreal Canadiens. At that point, history was hardly their ally. They were › PAGE 60

David Krejci scored in the first period of Game 1 at Philadelphia, setting the stage for a sweep.

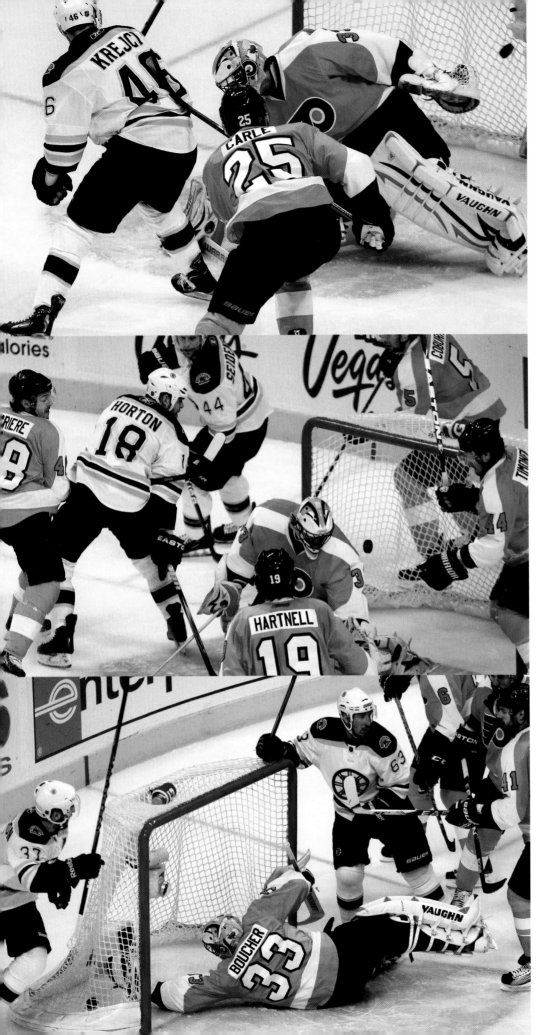

7-3

G A M E 1

David Krejci's first-period backhander past Flyers' goalie Brian Boucher was the start of a goal-scoring explosion by the Bruins in Game 1. Krejci had two of the Bruins' goals in a 7-3 rout, and was joined in the scoring column by Nathan Horton, who gave his team the lead for good with his first-period goal to make it 2-1. Patrice Bergeron (left) and Brad Marchand were on the doorstep of the Flyers' net to celebrate Mark Recchi's second-period goal as the onslaught continued.

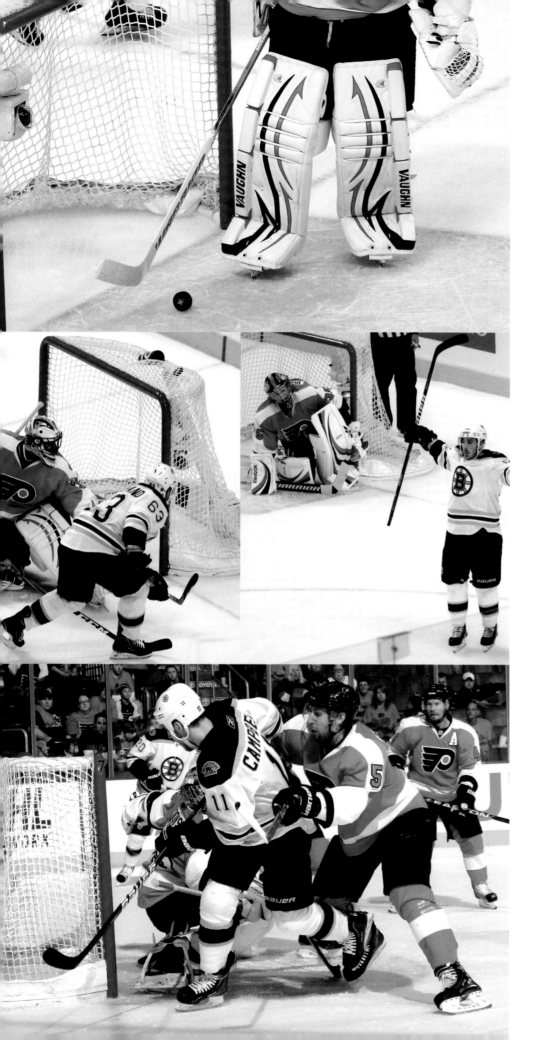

A beleaguered Brian Boucher (top) swept the puck out of the net following David Krejci's second goal. Things got worse for Boucher, who was helpless to stop the first of Brad Marchand's goals before being replaced in net by Sergei Bobrovsky. The new Flyers' goalie didn't fare much better, watching Marchand celebrate his third-period goal (middle right) before allowing Gregory Campbell's shot to sneak by (bottom), closing the scoring.

FROM 56 • constantly reminded that no Bruins team had extricated itself from an 0-2 hole, and never mind the events of a year ago, a disaster whose details appear to be known by every man, woman, child, and pet in the Commonwealth.

And now they have won eight of their last nine games and head to the Eastern Conference finals for the first time since 1992. This is precisely why sport is so vastly different from entertainment. You have to go out and play the game, and for the last two weeks the Bruins have been playing their best hockey of the year.

Save for that one Marchand gaffe, it was all good for the Boston Bruins in this Game 4. They started the evening with a stop-the-presses moment by scoring an honest-to-goodness, five-on-four goal, something that hasn't happened since gas was under three bucks a gallon (well, almost). And a

"WITH FIVE MINUTES LEFT, I LET MYSELF ... START TO THINK, 'HEY, THIS COULD BE IT; WE COULD WIN THIS GAME.' "

thing of beauty it was, too, as the puck was expertly passed from Bruin to Bruin before Milan Lucic took a pass from Nathan Horton and slipped it into a nice 3-foot gap to the left of Bobrovsky at 12:02 of the first period.

Thomas was not being overly taxed. The Bruins were the clear aggressors. Halfway through the second period they had an 18-9 shots-on-goal advantage, and that doesn't begin to tell the story, as there were 10 or more bullets that whizzed either left or right of the goaltender.

But all it takes in hockey is one goof to turn things around, and that is what happened when Marchand lost the puck

to Mike Richards and Versteeg made it 1-1 at the conclusion of the ensuing two-on-one rush with a nice move on Thomas, who really had no chance.

You can imagine the fan angst as the third period began. Losing this game would have been intolerable. But Boychuk relieved the pressure with a mighty blast that sailed over Bobrovsky's left shoulder.

"When it went in I felt relieved," said the 27-year old defenseman, whose shot is second on the Bruins only to Zdeno Chara's in terms of velocity. "The forward was coming at me very hard. I just shot a knuckler."

Watching from the other end of the ice was one very grateful goaltender.

"I was very happy, but I tried not to get too high because there was a lot of time left," Thomas said. "I didn't want to have that exhilaration, and then that crash."

The dam-burster came with a tick or two more than five minutes remaining. This time, it was Philadelphia's turn to lose the puck. Matt Carle gave it away to Horton, who has come alive at the most propitious juncture of the season. He held the puck, waited for Lucic to get a head of steam, slipped the puck to the rugged forward, and watched as Lucic sent one past Bobrovsky to make it 3-1.

Now Thomas could relax.

"When Looch scored the goal with five minutes left," Thomas said, "I let myself just a little start to, not celebrate, but start to think, 'Hey, this could be it; we could win this game.' "

Marchand scored an empty-netter at 18:04, if Thomas needed any more convincing.

There's a lot more hockey to come. But the Bruins can savor the fact that they annihilated a team that ruined their lives 12 months ago. Who could put a price on that? ⊚

Despite being down a game, Philadelphia fans assembled for Game 2 taunted Zdeno Chara with a reminder of Boston's epic collapse in last year's playoffs.

Back in goal for the Flyers in Game 2, Brian Boucher showed improvement but was late attempting this stick save on David Krejci's shot at 14:00 of overtime. Krejci's fourth goal of the postseason lifted the Bruins to a 3-2 victory and set off a team-wide celebration on the Wells Fargo Center ice. The Bruins stunned the Philadelphia faithful by leaving town with victories in the first two games of the series.

5-1

GAME 3

The Bruins knew they would get a more physical effort from the Flyers in Game 3 at the Garden, and were up to the challenge. Nathan Horton tangled with rugged Philadelphia defenseman Sean O'Donnell in a second-period fight, and Bruins defenseman Dennis Seidenberg (right) absorbed a major hit along the boards in the third period by Braydon Coburn. The Bruins dominated the game where it counts, registering a 5-1 victory to take a commanding 3-0 lead in the series. Not that anyone was feeling cocky after last year.

G A M E 4

The Bruins finished off their stunning series sweep of the Flyers with a second straight 5-1 romp, which brought smiles from coach Claude Julien and goalie Tim Thomas. But there was cause for concern regarding Patrice Bergeron (left), who had difficulty getting up from the ice following a third-period hit delivered by Claude Giroux. Bergeron did not return to the game and was diagnosed with a concussion, jeopardizing his availability for the Eastern Conference finals.

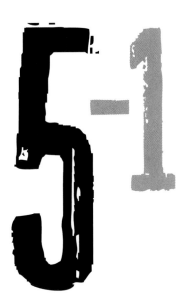

SHIRA SPRINGER / Globe Staff

JEREMY JACOBS OWNING HIS IMAGE

Sitting in the shadows of TD Garden, 20 rows from the ice, Jeremy Jacobs watched the Bruins practice for the Stanley Cup finals.

The out-of-town owner doesn't make "appearances," doesn't crave celebrity, doesn't see his role as cheerleader-in-chief. Of all Boston's major sports team owners, Jacobs, who purchased the Bruins in 1975 for $10 million, is the least visible and most restrained. Dressed in coat and tie, he spends playoff games pacing in a luxury box. The distance he keeps and the fact that his home is in East Aurora, New York, near Buffalo, largely account for his image as an aloof owner, someone too far removed from the Boston sports scene to truly value the Bruins' place in it.

Does he mind that people see him as disengaged? "That's obviously the image that I portray to them. I can't change that," said Jacobs. "... People who know me know my level of passion for my sport. Your actions have to speak louder."

Jacobs paused. "And apparently my actions haven't, my body language has sent the wrong signal. Hopefully, my body language now will change that."

Winning the NHL's ultimate prize gives the much-maligned Bruins owner a rare opportunity to remake his image. The Stanley Cup quiets longstanding critics who accuse Jacobs of caring more about the bottom line than winning, of viewing the Bruins as just another piece of his business empire, Delaware North Companies, which earns $2 billion in annual revenues from hospitality and food service.

"The image doesn't bear any relation to the real person that Jeremy Jacobs is," said NHL commissioner Gary Bettman. "No one I know is more passionate about the game of hockey and no owner more passionate about his team than he is. He is extraordinarily knowledgeable about the game and about the business of the game."

Still, Jacobs seems acutely aware of, even sensitive to, the criticism. He tries to convey the unique place the team holds in his portfolio, though sometimes it sounds like talking points more than passion.

"When you own a franchise in a city like Boston, these great, classic properties, it's not another asset," said Jacobs. "It's a civic asset that you're holding there. ... I didn't fully appreciate that until after I'd been there for several years. Then, it became more and more apparent that you were dealing with the emotions of a community and with the pride and the culture, more so than with anything else you would do."

Jacobs remains most comfortable behind the scenes, making almost daily calls to president Cam Neely and general manager Peter Chiarelli to discuss players, or solicit advice and opinions from his top executives. And sometimes to level a few quick hits with his dry sense of humor. ("He really likes to bust chops," said Neely.)

Jacobs will be the first to describe how his ownership style has "evolved," the first to acknowledge he could have handled relationships with the media better and been more available. But Jacobs came from a different school of ownership, when no one expected owners to be personalities.

"When you're dealing with a subject that you're not intimately day to day involved with, put competent people in charge and let them lead," Jacobs's father, Louis Jacobs, once told his son.

That hands-off philosophy is what Jacobs brought to the Bruins, where Harry Sinden, president of the Bruins for 17 years, was the man entrusted with the franchise. In 2006, what Jacobs calls a "watershed" year for the team, Jacobs brought in Chiarelli and Sinden moved into his senior adviser role. Coach Claude Julien and Neely arrived the next year. Jacobs said, in part, those changes were prompted by the insights of his son Charlie, who is the team's principal.

Jacobs sees the foundation for the Bruins' current success in the leadership of Neely, Chiarelli, and Julien. But he also sees something more valuable in the Bruins' current incarnation.

"I see sustainability," said Jacobs.

"This community will be hockey-frenzied for the next 15 years, not just now." ◉

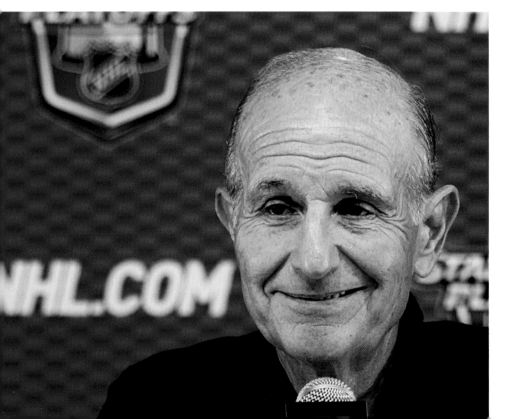

HARRY SINDEN HOW HE SEES IT

He is 78 years old now, a great-grandfather, and still a presence in the Bruins front office.

"They call me an adviser," Harry Sinden said recently when reached at his home north of Boston. "What I am is an observer. If they want, I give them my observations. Sometimes I give 'em to them even if they don't want 'em."

In more than 40 years of service with the team, as head coach, general manager, and "adviser," Sinden has always been the straightest of shooters. That has gotten him into trouble at times, and we thought maybe his bosses had locked him in the Garden basement this spring, but no. Sinden is still a vocal force in the Hub of Hockey. A few of his observations:

"I think [Tim] Thomas is the best goalie we've had since [Gerry] Cheevers. They're very similar in style. Tim is a little more athletic than Gerry. ... People ask me about him being unorthodox — how come I didn't hear those remarks about Dominik Hasek? This guy is a hell of a goalie.

"[Zdeno] Chara is just a terrific defenseman. We've had Bobby Orr and Brad Park and Raymond Bourque and now Chara. He's always one of the top two or three defensemen in the league.

"[Patrice] Bergeron is the type of player I like. He's like a Bobby Clarke or a Ronnie Francis, an all-around contributor. I like [David] Krejci, I like [Milan] Lucic. I like lots of them. They're good."

What does he think of his coach, the oft-maligned, stay-the-course Claude Julien?

"He's done a tremendous job," said Sinden. "There's a couple of aspects to coaching. You have to be able to communicate and you have to be able to get the players to play for you. He's done both of those things. These guys really want to play for him."

What about Peter Chiarelli, another guy who does a job Sinden used to do?

"We were weak at the back end of our lineup when he got here, and I think he's corrected that really well with guys like [Gregory] Campbell and [Chris] Kelly," said Sinden. "He's done a terrific job with guys like [Andrew] Ference on defense. He's supplemented this team and made it a Stanley Cup contender."

Sinden hoisted the Cup at City Hall Plaza when the Bruins were kings in 1970, but he has regrets about the near misses through the decades.

"There were disappointing times for everybody," he said. "We had a shot at winning it so many times. There was always a feeling, very much like with the Red Sox before '04. We ran up against a couple of dynasties with Edmonton, the Islanders, Montreal a couple of times."

Those near misses, coupled with Sinden's tight fiscal style, brought a big bowl of criticism to his doorstep. Looking back, he says he might do some things differently.

"It's very disappointing not to have won some championships with the teams we had, and I do have some regrets," he said. "Along with a couple of other teams in the NHL, we took on the players. We did what the league wanted us to do to prevent the lockout.

"Some teams didn't pay attention. We bore the brunt of that. We didn't sign free agents and we went to arbitration and walked away from players in arbitration. We did all the things the league wanted us to do in order to get the thing in financial order. In the end, I think we were the victims of that.

"But there are many things I would do the same. I had tremendous players. Everything starts with the players. You can talk about coaching and management and scouting, and they're all important, but it all starts with the players.

"That's why you have to give Claude Julien a lot of credit. This team has got what it takes. Do they have the same talent as the old Edmonton teams or the Islanders? Probably not. But they have that intangible. I've seen it in baseball and with the Celtics. Bobby Orr brought that kind of atmosphere here and I used to live in fear that we could lose that. Eventually, we did lose it, but this group has brought it back." ◉

The teams clashed for the 33d time in the playoffs (extending their NHL record), and Montreal leaped ahead, only to have the Bruins rally from an 0-2 playoff series deficit for the first time in their history.

CANADIENS BRUINS

Game 1

2-0

MON	1	0	1		2
BOS	0	0	0		0

THURSDAY, APRIL 14, 2011 • **BOSTON**

Game 2

3-1

MON	2	1	0		3
BOS	0	1	0		1

SATURDAY, APRIL 16, 2011 • **BOSTON**

Game 3

4-2

BOS	2	1	1		4
MON	0	1	1		2

MONDAY, APRIL 18, 2011 • **MONTREAL**

Game 4

5-4

BOS	0	3	1	1		5
MON	1	2	1	0		4

THURSDAY, APRIL 21, 2011 • **MONTREAL**

Game 5

2-1

MON	0	0	1	0	0		1
BOS	0	0	1	0	1		2

SATURDAY, APRIL 23, 2011 • **BOSTON**

Game 6

2-1

BOS	0	1	0		1
MON	1	1	0		2

TUESDAY, APRIL 26, 2011 • **MONTREAL**

Game 7

4-3

MON	1	1	1	0		3
BOS	2	0	1	1		4

WEDNESDAY, APRIL 27, 2011 • **BOSTON**

THEY HADN'T WON A GAME 7 OF ANY KIND SINCE 1994, when they played in the Old Garden and Boston had a new mayor named Tom Menino. THEY WERE ELIMINATED IN HEARTBREAKING GAME 7s each of the last three seasons, and there were questions about their hearts and souls when they took the ice for the final game of their 33d playoff series against the hated Montreal Canadiens. For one night, the Bruins made all the pain go away. No more agita on ice. Nathan Horton's booming slap shot in the sixth minute of overtime beat the Canadiens, 4-3, in Game 7 of their first-round playoff series at TD Garden. GAME 7. BRUINS-CANADIENS. OVERTIME. HOW MUCH BETTER DOES IT GET? Had the Bruins lost to the Canadiens, it could have been a franchise-altering defeat, with dire consequences for coach Claude Julien and general manager Peter Chiarelli. But this time the Bruins did not choke it away. Sure, they blew a 3-2 lead in the final two minutes of regulation,

R O U N D 1

and they failed to convert on a single power play for another night (0 for 21 for the series), but who cares when you win it in OT? These Bruins become the first team in franchise history (in 28 tries) to win a series after falling behind, two games to zero. GAME 7s HAVE NOT BEEN THE BRUINS' FRIENDS IN RECENT YEARS. The Pesky-Dent-Buckner-Boone torch has been passed to Zdeno Chara, Patrice Bergeron, and Andrew Ference. Julien has been in the Hub of Hockey for four years. His first three seasons ended in Game 7 defeats, the last two at home. Finally, he gets some relief and vindication. NOTHING COULD TOP THE ABJECT FAILURE OF THE 2010 BRUINS, who had a 3-0 series lead in the second round against the Flyers, saw the dominance fizzle as the Flyers won three straight, then came home to Causeway Street and lost, 4-3, after leading, 3-0. A 3-0 LEAD AT HOME IN A GAME 7 IS A LOCK … unless you are the Bruins. Those Bruins coughed up four consecutive goals and went home › PAGE 74

The Bruins celebrate their overtime win in Game 7.

FROM 72 • for a summer of speculation about their mental toughness.

This year's team had a lot of luggage to carry into the Jeremy Jacobs barn. The Garden rocked when the Bruins scored twice in the first seven minutes of Game 7 (a Johnny Boychuk slapper from just inside the blue line and a Mark Recchi wrist shot from the slot). What to think?

I don't know about you, but I was somewhat relieved that the Bruins weren't ahead by a prohibitive, unlucky 3-0.

Midway through the first, with the Bruins shorthanded, Canadiens defenseman Yannick Weber potted a goal on a wrist shot from the right side after Daniel Paille lost his stick — effectively making this another five-on-three goal for the Habs.

The Bruins failed to score on their 20th power play of the series at the end of the first. It had reached a point when the one-man-advantage for Boston was a decided disadvantage. You could almost see the Habs drooling at their prospects any time the Bruins went on the power play.

In the sixth minute of the second period, with the Bruins on the dreaded power play again, Montreal's Tomas Plekanec stole the puck from Recchi and went in alone on Boston goalie Tim Thomas. He did not miss. It was 2-2 and the Garden felt like a Temple of Doom. The Black and Gold were outshot, 12-7, in the second period.

We wondered if there was more torture in store for Bruins fans when Recchi fanned on an open net in the third. Then the Bruins struck. While Canadiens defenseman Roman Hamrlik lay on the ice, trying to sell a penalty after he was hit by Chris Kelly, the Bruins kept playing.

Andrew Ference fired a wrist shot that was blocked by Montreal goalie Carey Price, but Kelly was there for the nifty backhand rebound and a 3-2 lead with 10:16 left in the third.

The joy lasted until the final two minutes of regulation when Patrice Bergeron went off for high-sticking and Montreal defenseman P.K. Subban blasted a one-timer past Thomas for the 3-3 tie. Overtime.

Horton's slapper put the hockey universe back in order.

Neither one of these teams looked particularly Cup-worthy in this first round. The Bruins became the first team in NHL history to win a seven-game series without scoring on a power play. They will take plenty of baggage to Philadelphia.

But none of that matters. The Bruins played a Game 7 and did not choke. They sent the other guys home for the summer. Hockey lives in Boston in the spring of 2011.⊚

G A M E 1

Bruins goalie Tim Thomas
was on the losing end
of the game, and on
the wrong end of this
snow shower courtesy
of Montreal's Tomas
Plekanec. Thomas
saved 18 of 20 shots,
not good enough to
offset the stellar work of
his counterpart, Carey
Price, who stopped all 31
Bruins' shots to record
the shutout. There wasn't
much for Bruins coach
Claude Julien to feel good
about when he looked up
at the scoreboard in the
closing seconds (opposite
page). Brian Gionta scored
both goals for Montreal.

2-0

bok

GAME 2

Tim Thomas was a study in frustration as he watched the Canadiens celebrate following Yannick Weber's second-period goal. The B's had cut their deficit to one on Patrice Bergeron's goal, but Weber answered about 10 minutes later to close the scoring in the Canadiens' 3-1 victory, which gave them a 2-0 series lead. Bruins defenseman Dennis Seideneberg (below) was in the neighborhood for Weber's goal, and for Michael Cammalleri's first-period tally.

4-2

GAME 3

Players lunging, colliding, and crashing to the ice was a familiar sight in rough-and-tumble Game 3 as the series moved to Montreal. Almost in sequence during this second-period action, Patrice Bergeron and Brad Marchand of the Bruins and the Canadiens' James Wisniewski and P.K. Subban hit the deck while pursuing the puck. The all-out effort by the Bruins produced a 4-2 victory, cutting their series deficit to 2-1.

GAME 4

Michael Ryder fired the puck past goalie Carey Price at 1:59 of overtime to give the Bruins a 5-4 victory in Game 4. Patrice Bergeron had beaten Price with a second-period goal (above), and Chris Kelly forced the overtime by notching a third-period goal (right) with just 6:18 remaining. The Bruins deadlocked the series at two games apiece, continuing an unlikely trend in which the visiting team had won every game.

Brad Marchand barely missed sneaking the puck past an out-of-position Carey Price in the first overtime, but the Montreal goalie was not as fortunate in the second extra session as Nathan Horton potted the game-winner (below) in the Bruins' 2-1 victory, giving them their second straight overtime victory and first series lead.

2-1

GAME 6

Milan Lucic (below) earned an escort off the ice after drawing a game misconduct on his second-period boarding penalty. Lucic's ejection was part of a frustrating night for the Bruins at Bell Centre, summed up by defenseman Zdeno Chara's expression (right) following Michael Cammalleri's goal to open the scoring for Montreal. The Canadiens' 2-1 victory forced a deciding seventh game in Boston.

2-1

GAME 7

It took another overtime to get the job done, but David Krejci (46) and his teammates finally got past Carey Price when Nathan Horton's goal gave the Bruins a 4-3 victory in the seventh game of their Eastern Conference quarterfinal series. Chris Kelly (above) scored the third goal in the third period before P.K. Subban answered for the Canadiens, setting the stage for the dramatic overtime session and the celebration (left) that followed.

TIM THOMAS NET RESULTS

For goalies, the NHL is no place for snowflakes. It is a cookie-cutter league, now more than ever, one that prefers identical approaches over independent thinking. The preferred blueprint is that of Tuukka Rask: taller than 6 feet, flexible as Gumby, glove up, imposing even when down on his pads, most certainly playing the butterfly style.

Among that uniformity, the 5-foot-11-inch, 201-pound Tim Thomas is as unique as the white mask that protects his head (he prefers vertical bars instead of the universal cat's-eye design).

"I do play differently," said Thomas, "than just about anybody in the world."

His game, born from a battler's approach and a creative hockey mind, has made him the best goalie on Earth right now. That style, developed in six states (Michigan, Vermont, Alabama, Texas, Rhode Island, Massachusetts) and four countries (United States, Canada, Sweden, Finland), has more in common with a tornado than an efficient Swiss timepiece.

When a forward tiptoes into his crease, Thomas doesn't hesitate to chop him with his stick or step around him to get a better view of the play. If a shooter slashes into his slot, Thomas often employs a backstroke-like swim move to foil any second shot — he's assuming he'll stop the first — that might be coming. When a stray puck bobbles into his view and teammates are nowhere in sight, Thomas will go into a full swan dive to nudge it out of dangerous situations.

"Thinking outside the box," Thomas said. "I'm creative as far as finding different ways to get the job done. I might not necessarily have all the tools that other goalies have. But I'm willing to use my tools in creative ways."

In the fall of 1997, Thomas graduated from the University of Vermont and started his pro career. The hydrant-shaped goalie with the indescribable style had been selected by the Quebec Nordiques in the ninth round of the 1994 draft but was dismissed by what were then the Colorado Avalanche after his first pro training camp.

What scouts, coaches, and general managers saw was a helter-skelter scrambler. They didn't even see Thomas as having a technique. In their eyes, he was a goalie with an unheralded pedigree. To be less kind, a flopper.

Thomas disagreed. In 1997-98, while playing for HIFK Helsinki, he posted a 1.62 goals-against average and a .947 save percentage. Three years later, this time for Karpat, he had a 2.45 GAA and a .925 save percentage.

They were numbers that should have merited at least a sniff from NHL teams. But with limited viewings, scouts did not take a panoramic perspective of Thomas's performance.

"I do stuff that people don't associate with normal goaltending," he said. "It's one of my strengths. But if you're looking as a goaltending scout, I don't think they can stick their neck out to say that I'm going to be able to do it on a consistent basis. I think that's what they were saying earlier in my career."

So Thomas became a nomad. In the late 1990s, he played in Finland alongside future NHLers Olli Jokinen, Brian Rafalski, Jussi Jokinen, and Jarkko Ruutu. In 2004-05, during the NHL lockout, Brian Campbell and ex-Bruin Glen Metropolit were among Thomas's teammates.

"I have a well-rounded game," Thomas said. "I think every league I played in gave me a different discipline that I was exposed to."

In 2005-06, Thomas finally got his shot at age 31. He went 15-11-0 with a 2.26 GAA and a .923 save percentage for Scott Gordon's AHL team in Providence, then went unclaimed when he was recalled by Boston. The following season, the first under new management, Thomas went 30-29-4 with a 3.13 GAA and a .905 save percentage.

In the summer of 2007, when Dave Lewis was fired as Bruins coach after one season, Thomas had to win the confidence of a new man, Claude Julien.

"I've always been one of those guys that's said, 'As long as the goaltender stops the puck, I don't care,' I really don't," said Julien. "You can get these goaltenders that are technically sound, but they can't stop a puck.

"His compete level was there. At the same time, when I spoke to Timmy at the beginning, I said, 'My job is to make it easier on you as best I can by getting a good structure in front of you so you don't have to guess. You need to know how the players in front of you will react, which will help your style, too.'

"To me, he's been good every year. Last year, he had a good year. Not a great year. But a bit of that was the result of his health." (In the 2009-10 season, Thomas was slowed by wear and tear in his left hip that ultimately required surgery for a torn labrum.)

How good could Thomas have been had his NHL chance arrived earlier? Put him in the position of Rask, who was an NHL rookie at 22 last year. Plug in approximations of Thomas's performance, stretch them out over 15 or so seasons, and the numbers could challenge those of Martin Brodeur (612 wins, 114 shutouts).

Thomas hasn't given that much consideration. Instead, he combines his accomplishments to put his career into perspective.

"If I look back on all of those," he said, "then I think I've put together a record to be proud of personally." ⊚

> "I DO PLAY DIFFERENTLY THAN JUST ABOUT ANYBODY IN THE WORLD."

Tim Thomas was never better than during the playoffs, where more than once he showed he wasn't afraid to get physical and lay it all on the line. He also took time to reflect and celebrate. In the end, he made it all look easy.

Their regular season began with the two-game NHL Premiere series against the Phoenix Coyotes in Prague, and ended six months later against the Devils in New Jersey. In between, despite bumps, the Bruins served notice that the team would be a major player in the Eastern Conference in 2010-11.

OCTOBER
6-2-0

After losing the opener, Boston blanked Phoenix on the back end of the series in Prague, 3-0, beginning a four-game winning streak. They closed the month with shutout victories over Toronto and Ottawa.

JANUARY
8-4-2

New Year's Day did not result in any celebrating for the Bruins in a 7-6 shootout loss to the Sabres, but they rebounded to beat the Maple Leafs two days later, and finished the month with victories in seven of 10 games.

APRIL
3-2-0

With the playoffs on the horizon, the Bruins scored victories over the Thrashers, Islanders, and Senators. Their loss to the Devils in the finale took nothing away from an impressive 103-point campaign.

NOVEMBER
6-6-2

Not a stellar month for the Bruins, but they still managed to record three straight victories in Eastern Conference matchups against the Devils, Rangers, and Panthers.

FEBRUARY
8-4-0

Boston's most productive month began with three straight victories and ended with five straight, the latter streak including a 3-1 victory over the Canucks in Vancouver. A sign of things to come.

DECEMBER
8-3-3

Boston began with victories over Philadelphia and Tampa Bay, the teams they would see in the Eastern Conference semifinals and finals. The Bruins also beat the Lightning later in the month as part of a Florida sweep that included a shootout victory over the Panthers the day before.

MARCH
7-4-4

Carrying the momentum of their February winning streak, the Bruins began the month with victories over the Senators and Lightning. They slumped to lose four in a row and six of seven before rediscovering their touch with victories in four of their next five.

2010/2011 EASTERN CONFERENCE

NORTHEAST	W	L	OT	PTS
Boston	46	25	11	103*
Montreal	44	30	8	96
Buffalo	43	29	10	96
Toronto	37	34	11	85
Ottawa	32	40	10	74

*The Bruins had five OT losses and six shootout losses. (Their 103-point total reflects two points for each win, plus 11 points, one for each OT or shootout loss.)

CHEERS & JEERS & JEERS

VERSUS EVERYBODY

FOR THOSE WHO CARE, AND THEY CAN BE COUNTED ON FINGERS AND TOES, the score of the final Bruins game of the regular season was 3-2 at the Prudential Center in Newark. The rumor was that the Devils won. "Just one of those games where you're glad it's out of the way," said Bruins coach Claude Julien when it was over. His focus immediately turned to the playoffs, which once again meant squaring off with the Canadiens. No other clubs have played each other as often (33 times, and counting) in the postseason.

TWO YEARS AGO, THE BRUINS BOOTED THE CANADIENS IN FOUR GAMES. In 2007-08, Julien's first year at the helm, the upstart Bruins engaged the Canadiens in a seven-game dogfight before bowing out in the first round.

S E A S O N

The rivalry required no further stoking. But this season, tempers flared white hot. P.K. Subban flattened Brad Marchand with an open-ice wallop December 16. On February 9, during an 8-6 Boston win, there were six fights, including a center-ice throwdown between goaltenders Tim Thomas and Carey Price.

"THE HATRED IS DEFINITELY THERE AGAIN," Bruins forward Milan Lucic said. "That's what makes this game fun. That's why it's great to be part of this rivalry." The boiling point came March 8. That night at the Bell Centre, Zdeno Chara drove Max Pacioretty into a stanchion. Pacioretty was diagnosed with a fractured vertebra and a severe concussion that put him out for the rest of the season.

AFTER CHARA ESCAPED SUSPENSION — he was tagged with an interference major and a game misconduct that night — Montreal fans went into a tizzy. They called 911, demanding Chara be cuffed and booked. The Montreal police opened an investigation. Air Canada threatened to yank its sponsorship unless the league addressed head shots.

UPON ALL THIS, Mark Recchi unleashed a steady stream of gasoline. On March 23, during a 98.5 WBZ-FM interview, Recchi hinted that the › PAGE 95

CZECH MATE
10/3/10

Far away from home, the Bruins opened the season in Prague with a pair of games against the Phoenix Coyotes. Not so far away from home, Slovakian-born Bruins' captain Zdeno Chara and Czech teammate David Krejci posed in front of the NHL Premiere poster that greeted their arrival overseas. The Bruins lost the opener, 5-2, and won the second game, 3-0.

ONE TO WATCH
10/28/10

Rookie Tyler Seguin gave Bruins' fans a glimpse of his offensive skills in a 2-0 victory at TD Garden, beating Toronto goalie Jonas Gustavsson (right) for his second goal of the season. Seguin celebrated with teammates afterward.

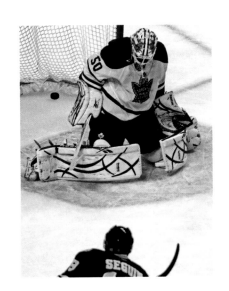

FROM 92 · Canadiens had embellished the severity of Pacioretty's injuries in hopes of getting Chara suspended.

The next day, after a 7-0 thumping of the Canadiens, Recchi said he had made his flammable comments to take the heat off his captain.

In their final game before the playoffs, the Bruins stamped a bookend on a regular season that started in Prague. They ended the year in third place in the Eastern Conference, a respectable finish given the absence of Marc Savard, their ace playmaker.

There were other positives. Rich Peverley and Chris Kelly, acquired from Atlanta and Ottawa, respectively, to firm up the roster, scored the Boston goals. Tim Thomas broke Dominik Hasek's all-time save percentage record. Chara placed himself in the conversation for a second Norris Trophy. Lucic busted the 30-goal mark. Brad Marchand blossomed from fourth-line energy forward to a top-six, all-around threat. For the fourth straight year under Julien, the Bruins qualified for the playoffs.

"There were a lot of things we accomplished," Julien said. "Defensively, always at the top of the league. Offensively, I think we're fifth. We accomplished a lot. Our power play is the thing people have talked the most about. Hopefully we get that going in the right direction in the playoffs and it makes a difference."

"Lot of good things our team accomplished this year. When you look at the whole season, our team was climbing and climbing and climbing. There wasn't too many times when it took a dip. Or if it did, it wasn't a long dip. It was pretty consistent, although people seem to see it a different way. You look around, there were probably a lot of teams that had bigger dips than we did. I'm trying to stay positive and look at the positive things."

His players were also looking on the bright side, and looking ahead. "The two games we won in Boston, we just played," said Lucic. "That's what we're going to have to do — play our game and skate. I think when we're moving our feet, skating well with the puck, and making plays at high speed, that's when we're most effective." ◎

HARD DAZE
1/22/11
The Bruins' season was filled with magical moments, but also had its trials and tribulations. Marc Savard, one of the NHL's best playmaking centers, sustained his second concussion in less than a year on Jan. 22 at the hands of Colorado's Matt Hunwick. Weeks later, a forlorn Savard was left to ponder his future while sitting at a press conference on Feb. 7 in which general manager Peter Chiarelli announced he would sit out the remainder of the season.

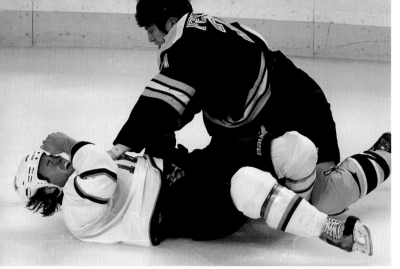

FIGHT CLUB
2/3/11

As always, the season had a heaping helping of big-time bouts, including Andrew Ference's unanimous decision against Adam Burish (above left), and a slugfest between Gregory Campbell and Steve Ott in which goalie Tim Thomas enjoyed his ringside seat (above right). Both dustups were part of a game against Dallas at TD Garden that featured three fights in the first four seconds. Campbell's face told the story of a hard-nosed game won by the Bruins, 6-3.

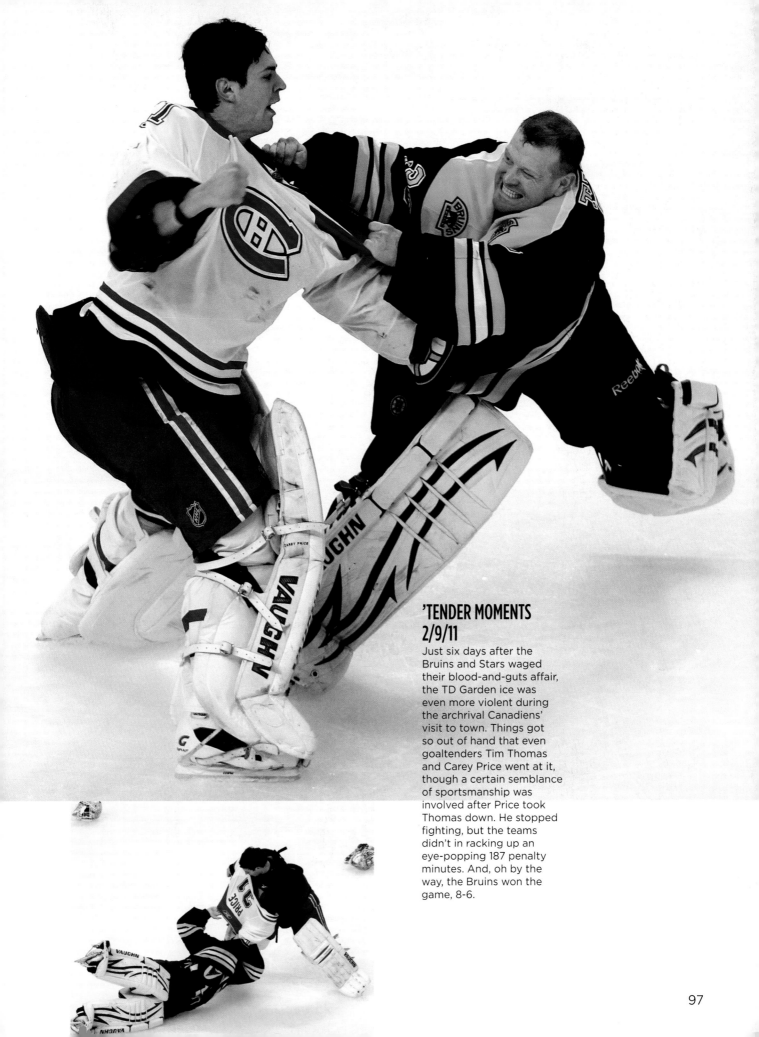

'TENDER MOMENTS
2/9/11

Just six days after the Bruins and Stars waged their blood-and-guts affair, the TD Garden ice was even more violent during the archrival Canadiens' visit to town. Things got so out of hand that even goaltenders Tim Thomas and Carey Price went at it, though a certain semblance of sportsmanship was involved after Price took Thomas down. He stopped fighting, but the teams didn't in racking up an eye-popping 187 penalty minutes. And, oh by the way, the Bruins won the game, 8-6.

Not known for a physical style of play, Tomas Kaberle demonstrated he could dish out punishment every now and then. He took down Manny Malhotra of the Canucks during the Bruins' 3-1 victory in Vancouver on Feb. 26. Kaberle also contributed to the offense with an assist. Three months later, these teams would be back at it with much higher stakes involved.

POWERING UP
2/18/11

The Bruins hoped to bolster their power play when they acquired playmaking defenseman Tomas Kaberle from the Toronto Maple Leafs. Traded for the first time in his 12-year NHL career, Kaberle barely had time to get acquainted with his new teammates — other recent additions included Rich Peverley and Chris Kelly — before taking the ice in Ottawa for warm-ups.

AWAY TEAM
2/17–3/1/11

The Feb. 26 win in Vancouver was part of a perfect six-game road trip that lifted the Bruins heading into March. Their run began on Feb. 17, when Islanders goalie Nathan Lawson (below) was left to watch Daniel Paille and Shawn Thornton celebrate Gregory Campbell's goal in a 6-3 victory in New York. Tomas Kaberle (right) kept a close eye on the Flames' Tim Jackman during a 3-1 victory in Calgary on Feb. 22. Milan Lucic of the Bruins and Jim Vandermeer of the Oilers (below right) traded punches in the third period of a 3-2 victory on Feb. 27 in Edmonton. In pursuit of the puck, Patrice Bergeron (far right) bowled over the

Senators' Bobby Butler during the Bruins' 1-0 victory on March 1 in Ottawa, where Boston had also won a 4-2 decision on Feb. 18. Nathan Horton celebrated with teammates (far right, below) after scoring the lone goal in the third period.

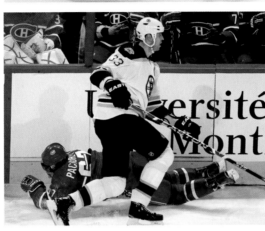

THE HIT 3/8/11

The hit heard around Canada came at Bell Centre as Zdeno Chara delivered a bone-crushing check on Max Pacioretty at 19:44 of the second period. The force of Chara's check sent Pacioretty headfirst into a glass stanchion, after which he lay motionless. Pacioretty suffered a concussion and fractured vertebra. Habs fans called 911 asking for a criminal investigation. Chara's sentence was a major penalty for interference and a game misconduct.

THE HIT MAN
3/24/11
While his hit on Max Pacioretty did not result in a fine or suspension from the league, Zdeno Chara remained a wanted man in Montreal. His popularity in Boston was never in question, however, as demonstrated by the warm runway greeting he received from TD Garden fans en route to the ice before the Bruins and Canadiens met again on March 24. The Bruins won easily, 7-0.

ALISON O'LEARY / Globe Correspondent

One man has started more games for the Boston Bruins than anyone else and outlasted stars like Ray Bourque and Cam Neely with his tux immaculate and nary a hair out of place. He's Rene Rancourt, a Natick, Massachusetts resident who has sung "The Star-Spangled Banner" at the opening of Bruins games for some 30 years.

Rancourt's anthem-singing in Boston actually began at Fenway Park, soon after he won an opera audition competition that was broadcast on the radio and heard by the late John Kiley, who was a longtime Boston Garden and Fenway Park organist. And the biggest event of his career also took place in Fenway, when he was called to fill in for the late singer Kate Smith, who had canceled her appearance just hours before the dramatic sixth game of the 1975 World Series between the Cincinnati Reds and the Boston Red Sox.

Nate Greenberg, assistant to Bruins president Harry Sinden, remembers that Rancourt was hired in 1976 on the strength of his voice. "We tried a couple of other people, but no one worked out very well. The problem was that the sound system in the Boston Garden was horrid, and none of them had voices that carried. ... He had a booming voice."

While he may also be heard at local youth sports events or kicking off an auto race in New Hampshire, Rancourt is in his element when the carpet is rolled onto the ice and, with opposing teams watching, he briefly steps into the spotlight.

The minute-long performances have added up over the years, until his name is readily identified with the black and gold of Boston's hockey tradition. He's the only person named in the punk rock group Dropkick Murphys' ode to Bruins games, a rollicking tune called "Time to Go."

And he notes that he'll always be part of Bruins trivia as the only national anthem singer to contribute indirectly to a player's injury, when Bruin Bob Joyce separated his shoulder tripping over the carpet placed on the ice for Rancourt.

Rancourt thrives on the thunderous applause that signals readiness for the opening puck drop of a NHL game. He puts his mark on his performances by pumping his fist at the end of the anthem, a gesture he said he picked up from Bruins player Randy Burridge. But even after 30 years of performing before huge crowds, it's still a nerve-racking challenge to sing the national anthem.

"I'm never comfortable singing it," he said. "If there's anything wrong with you, it will show in the song. I very rarely get it right, and that's why I like it. The challenge is very stimulating. There have been maybe 10 times in my career when I think I sang it really well." ⊕

"I'M NEVER COMFORTABLE SINGING IT."

Rene Rancourt has had his moments at Fenway (far left) and elsewhere. But he's best known for bringing a bit of Vegas to 30 years of singing the National Anthem before Bruins games, including the signature fist pump he picked up from former Bruin Randy Burridge.

With six Stanley Cups in 18 trips to the finals, the Bruins are no strangers to the winners' circle. Their biggest stars' numbers have been retired to the Garden rafters. But many more have won our hearts, even if they never hoisted the Cup here.

Bobby Orr was a face in the crowd when his moment of flight was immortalized with a bronze statue outside TD Garden 40 years after his Stanley Cup-winning goal.

GLORY DAYS

1924/25

1925/26

1926/27- 1931/32

1932/33-1933/34

2007/08-PRESENT

BY KEVIN PAUL DUPONT/ Globe Staff

The old Boston Garden, its sightlines steep and ideal for hockey, opened in 1928. But the Bruins were a success with the Boston sporting public even before moving into their new rink above the rumbling trains of North Station.

1934/35-1947/48

1948/49

1949/50-1994/95

1995/96-2006/07

Owned by grocery store magnate Charles F. Adams, and with Art
Ross the coach and general manager, the Boston Professional Hockey
Association Inc. had routinely packed fans into Boston Arena. The
Roaring Twenties were in full swing when C.F. Adams plunked down his
$15,000 and bought the NHL's first American franchise. › PAGE 110

1929

FROM 109 · Chicago, Detroit, and New York all entered in '26. The Celtics wouldn't be born for another 20-plus years when the Bruins christened the franchise against the Montreal Maroons on December 1, 1924. The Red Sox already were six years into a World Series victory drought that would last awhile. And Billy Sullivan, his Boston Patriots not born until 1960, hadn't yet learned how to dial his first lawyer.

Hockey in the Hub became instantly hot, a sport that captivated audiences with its spirited contact and its condoned — if not encouraged — brawling. Scores were low in the early days, but fists were often high. On top of it all, the Bruins were operating in the economic winter wonderland of what amounted to a sports entertainment monopoly.

There was even a night (November 15, 1927), before they moved to the Garden, when ex-Red Sox lefthander Babe Ruth sat in the Arena and watched the Bruins and Black Hawks battle to a 1-1 tie.

"Never saw anything like it," said the Bambino, treated to some ferocious hitting that evening by Bruins defenseman Eddie Shore. "Thank God I'm in baseball, with its peace and quiet."

The Bruins' early years in the Garden brought them three Stanley Cups in a little more than a decade ('29, '39 and '41). A night in the Garden to see the Bruins play then was akin somewhat to going to the theater. Men wore suits and hats. Women wore dresses. It was an occasion, an event to see the likes of Shore and Cecil "Tiny" Thompson and later the fabled "Kraut Line" —Milt Schmidt, Bobby Bauer,

Goaltender Tiny Thompson and defenseman Eddie Shore (2) led the Bruins to Stanley Cups in 1929 and 1939.

1929

Dit Clapper, the only Bruin to play on three championship teams.

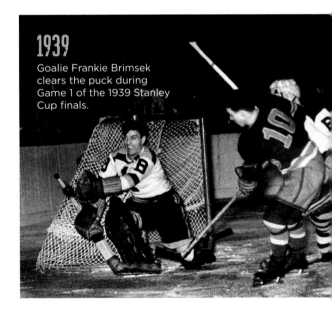

1939
Goalie Frankie Brimsek clears the puck during Game 1 of the 1939 Stanley Cup finals.

1939 All three members of the legendary "Kraut Line," (left to right) Woody Dumart, Bobby Bauer, and Milt Schmidt, are in the Hall of Fame.

and Woody Dumart. It was a respectable crowd, dotted here and there with lockjawed Boston Brahmins out to see what was sometimes a nasty night of entertainment. The most loyal of the fans, the Gallery Gods, sat in the cheapest seats in the house.

They were rewarded on April 16, 1939, when the Bruins pinned a 3-1 loss on the Maple Leafs to win the first of two Cups (the other in 1970) they would seal on Causeway Street. Shore, who had retreated to the locker room after the final whistle, was summoned back by the chanting crowd. "And when Edward Shore skated out on to that ice," recalled Schmidt, "the ovation that man received ... I can still hear it and feel it."

Shore played only four more games in a Bruins uniform after the '39 Cup win, finishing out his career in 1940. His departure followed by the start of World War II dealt the Bruins two devastating blows.

Boston netminder Frank Brimsek lost two seasons to the war. The Krauts each gave up three-plus seasons, departing en masse for the duration on February 11, 1942, one of the most memorable evenings in franchise history. The Bruins smacked around the Habs, 8-1, and the line of Schmidt, Bauer, and Dumart divvied up half of the evening's 22 points. When it was over, the Krauts were called to center ice, where they were presented with gifts and paychecks, and ultimately carried around the Garden on the shoulders of the Canadiens.

The classy Montrealers went on to win a pair of Cups by the spring of '46. The Bruins, who had won the Cup 10 months before

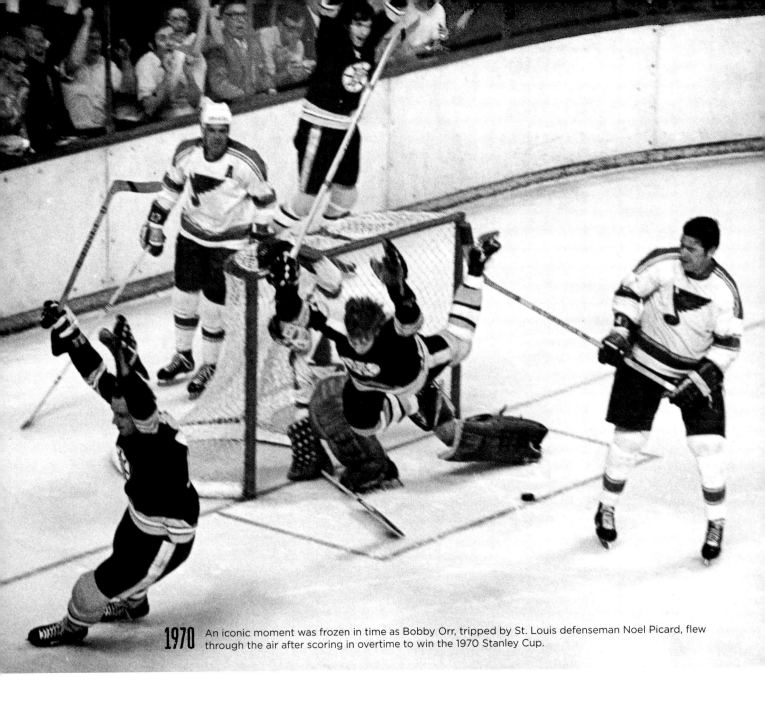

1970 An iconic moment was frozen in time as Bobby Orr, tripped by St. Louis defenseman Noel Picard, flew through the air after scoring in overtime to win the 1970 Stanley Cup.

1970

Phil Esposito, Fred Stanfield, and Gary Doak (left to right) enjoyed the taste of victory in 1970.

1970

Fans lined the city streets for a raucous parade honoring Bobby Orr, waving, and his teammates after they won the Cup.

the Krauts' departure, wouldn't win another until 1970.

"Mr. Art Ross gave us a Royal Canadian Air Force pilot's watch that night," recalled Schmidt. "To this day, I've never understood how the thing works."

The Bruins made it to the finals only once more in the '40s (a 4-1 series loss to the Canadiens in '46), and three times in the '50s (three more losses to the Canadiens in '53, '57 and '58). Following a defeat to Toronto in the '59 semifinals, Boston went a franchise-worst eight straight seasons without qualifying for the postseason.

Attendance at the Garden was respectable, the hard-core season ticket-holders remained faithful, but interest in a crowded sports market was waning. The Sox still hadn't won since Ruth was sold to the Yanks, but now the Celtics and Patriots were vying for attention and the public's disposable income. The Bruins had Willie O'Ree, the first black player in the NHL, and the Uke Line of Vic Stasiuk, Bronco Horvath and John Bucyk, but overall the mid-'50s and mid-'60s were glum days.

Then came Bobby Orr.

"I have this saying," said Schmidt, who was the Bruins' head coach at the start of the '60s, when the club began scouting Orr as a 12-year-old in Parry Sound, Ontario. "If anybody else comes along that's better than Orr, I hope the Good Lord sees fit to keep me on this earth to watch him — because he will be something else."

It was Orr's arrival in the fall of '66, along with the May 15, 1967, trade with Chicago for Phil Esposito, Ken Hodge, and Fred Stanfield, that brought the Bruins back to days of

1972

The Bruins let a 5-1 cushion slip away in Game 1 of the finals against the New York Rangers before Ace Bailey came to the rescue, beating Ed Giacomin to score the winning goal in the waning moments.

1972 In Game 3, Wayne Cashman (top) was denied by Giacomin and the Bruins lost, 5-2. But Boston rallied to win the series in Game 6, igniting a memorable party at City Hall.

glory. This time the fervor exceeded even that of the earlier Cup years. With the young Harry Sinden their coach, the swashbuckling and talented Bruins piled up scoring records, with Orr skating and contributing on offense like no defenseman in the history of the game. The Bruins of the late '60s and early '70s were a special team.

Night after night, crazed fans packed the Garden to see Orr and Espo, Derek (Turk) Sanderson and Johnny (Pie) McKenzie, the heroics of Gerry (Cheesie) Cheevers behind his mock-stitched goalie's mask.

"Jesus Saves," read the most popular bumper sticker of the day, "and Espo scores on the rebound." The Garden was a church and the Bruins the deities.

On May 10, 1970, Sanderson and Orr teamed up for the most memorable goal in the franchise's history. Tied with the St. Louis Blues, 3-3, in overtime at Boston Garden, Orr fed a pass to Sanderson in the right corner and cut out of the faceoff circle to collect Sanderson's pass and knock it by goalie Glenn Hall for the Bruins' first Cup since '41. The picture of Orr flying through the air, upended by defenseman Noel Picard, lives on in memories and on barroom walls across New England.

Two years later, the Bruins won the Cup again, this time at Madison Square Garden. But time, the rival World Hockey Association and NHL expansion already were conspiring, all poised to cripple Boston's dreams for more Cups. There have been good days since, including trips to the finals in 1988 and '90. The Bruins got a new arena in 1995. But the days of Orr and the old Garden euphoria have never been repeated.

Until now.⊚

CLOSE CALLS · A FEW WHO FELL JUST SHORT

It was Guy Lafleur and the Montreal Canadiens in 1977 and '78. Edmonton's Mark Messier did the honors in 1990. And if not for a power failure during the 1988 finals, Wayne Gretzky might have paraded the Stanley Cup around Boston Garden ice.

Present company excluded, the Bruins reached five finals after 1972, only to come up empty against some of the greatest teams in NHL history.

They were favored to defeat the Philadelphia Flyers in 1974, but not even Bobby Orr and Phil Esposito could prevent a 1-0 shutout at the hands of goalie Bernie Parent in a Cup-clinching Game 6.

A vastly different roster took on mighty Montreal in 1977. The colorful Don Cherry was behind the bench, and

the stars were Terry O'Reilly, Brad Park, and Jean Ratelle. But the Canadiens, losers of only eight regular season games, predictably swept the Bruins. A rematch the following spring didn't go much better. Although the Bruins fought back from a 2-0 deficit to deadlock the series, they dropped consecutive 4-1 affairs to fall short once more.

It was déjà vu all over again against the Canadiens in 1979, this time in the Eastern Conference finals. The closing two minutes of regulation in Game 7 at the Montreal Forum are among the most gut-wrenching in franchise history. A Bruins' penalty for too many men on the ice led to Lafleur's game-tying goal, and the Canadiens won in overtime.

With Ray Bourque and Cam Neely leading the way, the Bruins finally ended

the Canadiens' curse en route to the 1988 finals, defeating their hated rivals in the playoffs for the first time in 45 years. Still, they were no match for Edmonton, losing in four straight. The most memorable moment was the Boston Garden blackout that forced suspension of Game 4. The series shifted to Edmonton, where the Oilers completed the sweep.

The Oilers derailed Boston's hopes once again two years later. The opening game at the Garden was the longest in finals history, stretching into triple overtime. Edmonton's Petr Klima won the game at 15:13 of the third OT, and the Bruins never recovered, dropping the series in five. It would be 21 long years before the Stanley Cup finals returned to Boston. ⊛

In the Great Blackout of 1988 (above left), Boston Garden went dark during Game 4 of the finals against Edmonton, forcing play to be suspended. At right (from top) franchise legends Terry O'Reilly, Ray Bourque, and Cam Neely each played in two finals, but never got their hands on the Stanley Cup as members of the Bruins. Bourque eventually held aloft the silver chalice after being traded to Colorado.

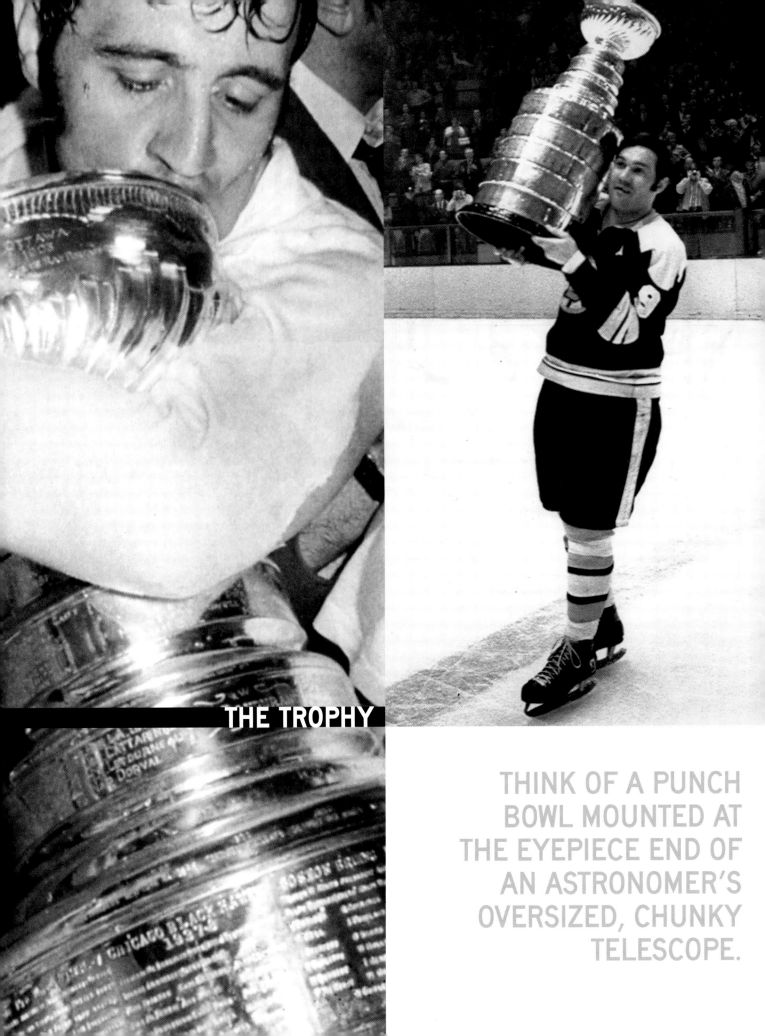

THE TROPHY

THINK OF A PUNCH BOWL MOUNTED AT THE EYEPIECE END OF AN ASTRONOMER'S OVERSIZED, CHUNKY TELESCOPE.

KEVIN PAUL DUPONT
Globe Staff

Bearded, worn-out, grizzled men alternately whoop and whimper at its sight.

By far the most recognized trophy in all of North American sports, and among the most identifiable throughout the world, the Stanley Cup inspires greatness, summons tears, and perhaps most of all, represents the crowning achievement of what is arguably the hardest, most grueling championship to win.

Today's version of the Cup weighs 34 1/2 pounds and is 35 1/4 inches high. Think of a punch bowl mounted at the eyepiece end of an astronomer's oversized, chunky telescope. The bowl was a gift from England, presented in 1894 to Canada's best amateur hockey team, the Montreal Amateur Athletic Association. Great Britain's Governor General to Canada, Sir Frederick Arthur Stanley of Preston, was the father of the idea, and purchased the bowl for 10 guineas — a sum of slightly less than $50 at the time — from a silversmith in London.

The original punch bowl, lined in gold, measured 7 1/2 inches high and 11 1/2 inches across, and was retired to a vault in the Hockey Hall of Fame in Toronto in the late 1960s after it became too old and brittle to be lugged safely from hockey barn to hockey barn. It is permanently housed in a glass display case in the HHOF museum, along with a number of the retired bands that bear the engraved names of the Cup's winners through the decades.

When the bottom of the five largest bands that form the Cup's base fills up with names, the top band is removed — retired to the vault — and a blank band added at the bottom for the names of future Cup winners. The other four bands shingle up, closer to the hallowed Cup. The current bottom band, which will have the Bruins' names etched in it this summer by official engraver Louise St. Jacques, began with the 2004-05 season, the only NHL season entirely lost to job action (owners' lockout). It reads, "Season Cancelled."

Once the Cup is clinched, it almost immediately goes on tour, each player

A CUP OF DREAMS

of the winning team granted his day with it in the city of his choosing. In 2001 ex-Boston captain/icon Ray Bourque brought his Colorado Cup to Boston City Hall for a crowd of thousands to share his joy. Otherwise, the Cup hasn't taken a bow in the Hub of Hockey since 1972.

"It's been that one piece missing for a while now. People are waiting for it," Bruins wingman Mark Recchi said during the 2011 playoffs. "... We want to give it to 'em." ☺

It's had its day with (left to right) Phil Esposito, Johnny Bucyk, and Harry Sinden. Now the Stanley Cup will be cuddled and coveted by a whole new generation of Bruins players and coaches.

Bobby Orr (left) and Terry O'Reilly (right) helped Milt Schmidt off the ice after the trio of Bruins legends skated at Fenway Park during festivities at the 2010 Winter Classic.

FORWARDS

37
PATRICE BERGERON
Ancienne-Lorette, Quebec, CAN

HT	WT	DOB
6' 2"	194	07-24-1985

11
GREGORY CAMPBELL
London, Ontario, CAN

HT	WT	DOB
6' 0"	197	12-17-1983

18
NATHAN HORTON
Welland, Ontario, CAN

HT	WT	DOB
6' 2"	229	05-29-1985

23
CHRIS KELLY
Toronto, Ontario, CAN

HT	WT	DOB
6' 0"	198	11-11-1980

46
DAVID KREJCI
Sternberk, CZE

HT	WT	DOB
6' 0"	177	04-28-1986

17
MILAN LUCIC
Vancouver, BC, CAN

HT	WT	DOB
6' 4"	220	06-07-1988

63
BRAD MARCHAND
Halifax, Nova Scotia, CAN

HT	WT	DOB
5' 9"	183	05-11-1988

20
DANIEL PAILLE
Welland, Ontario, CAN

HT	WT	DOB
6' 0"	200	04-15-1984

49
RICH PEVERLEY
Kingston, Ontario, CAN

HT	WT	DOB
6' 0"	195	07-08-1982

28
MARK RECCHI
Kamloops, BC, CAN

HT	WT	DOB
5' 10"	195	02-0

73
MICHAEL RYDER
Bonavista, NL, CAN

HT	WT	DOB
6' 0"	186	03-31-1980

91
MARC SAVARD
Ottawa, Ontario, CAN

HT	WT	DOB
5' 10"	191	07-17-1977

19
TYLER SEGUIN
Brampton, Ontario, CAN

HT	WT	DOB
6' 1"	182	01-31-1992

22
SHAWN THORNTON
Oshawa, Ontario, CAN

HT	WT	DOB
6' 2"	217	07-23-1977

DEFENSEMEN

43
MATT BARTKOWSKI
Pittsburgh, PA, USA

HT	WT	DOB
6' 1"	196	06-04-1988

55
JOHNNY BOYCHUK
Edmonton, Alberta, CAN

HT	WT	DOB
6' 2"	225	01-19-1984

33
ZDENO CHARA
Trencin, SVK

HT	WT	DOB
6' 9"	255	03-18-1977

21
ANDREW FERENCE
Edmonton, Alberta, CAN

HT	WT	DOB
5' 11"	189	03-17-1979

34
SHANE HNIDY
Neepawa, Manitoba, CAN

HT	WT	DOB
6' 2"	204	11-08-1975

12
TOMAS KABERLE
Rakovnik, CZE

HT	WT	DOB
6' 1"	214	03-02-1978

47
STEVEN KAMPFER
Ann Arbor, MI, USA

HT	WT	DOB
5' 11"	197	09-24-1988

54
ADAM McQUAID
Charlottetown, PE, CAN

HT	WT	DOB
6' 4"	197	10-12-1986

44
DENNIS SEIDENBERG
Schwenningen, DEU

HT	WT	DOB
6' 1"	210	07-18-1981

GOALIES

35
ANTON KHUDOBIN
Ust-Kamenogorsk, KAZ

HT	WT	DOB
5' 11"	203	05-07-1986

40
TUUKKA RASK
Savonlinna, Finland

HT	WT	DOB
6' 3"	169	03-10-1987

30
TIM THOMAS
Flint, MI, USA

HT	WT	DOB
5' 11"	201	04-15-1974

COACH

CLAUDE JULIEN
Blind River, Ontario, CAN

DOB
04-23-1960

2010/2011 REGULAR SEASON

DATE	OPPONENT		SCORE		PLACE	UP/DOWN	NOTABLE
10-9	Phoenix (@Prague)	L	5-2		4th	-4	Local hero Radim Vrbata scored twice to lead Coyotes.
10-10	Phoenix (@Prague	W	3-0		2nd	-2	Nathan Horton tallied third goal in two games.
10-16	@New Jersey	W	4-1		3rd	-4	Rookie Jordan Caron pocketed first NHL goal.
10-19	@Washington	W	3-1		3rd	-3	Tim Thomas made 35 saves as exhausting road trip concluded.
10-21	Washington	W	4-1		2nd	-1	Thomas's 38 saves and Horton's fourth goal led in home opener.
10-23	NY Rangers	L	3-2		3rd	-1	Marc Staal's breakaway snapped Bruins' four-game winning streak.
10-28	Toronto	W	2-0		3rd	-3	Tyler Seguin thrilled Garden crowd with first goal.
10-30	@Ottawa	W	4-0		2nd	-3	Thomas improved to 6-0 with second straight shutout.
11-3	@Buffalo	W	5-2		2nd	-1	Brad Marchand and Michael Ryder each collected two points.
11-5	@Washington	L	5-3		2nd	-3	Bruins erased three-goal deficit before losing.
11-6	St. Louis	O(SO)	1-1		2nd	-2	Bruins hit four posts in shootout defeat.
11-10	@Pittsburgh	W	7-4		2nd	-2	Five-goal third period stunned Penguins.
11-11	Montreal	L	3-1		2nd	-4	Carey Price (34 saves) stoned Bruins.
11-13	Ottawa	L	2-0		3rd	-6	Senators handed Thomas first loss.
11-15	New Jersey	W	3-0		2nd	-4	Thomas rebounded with fourth shutout.
11-17	@NY Rangers	W	3-2		2nd	-4	Bruins improved to 7-1 on the road.
11-18	Florida	W	4-0		2nd	-2	Tuukka Rask made 41 saves in first win.
11-20	Los Angeles	O(SO)	3-3		2nd	-3	Kings prevailed in sixth round of shootout.
11-22	@Tampa Bay	L	3-1		2nd	-3	Steven Stamkos scored league-leading 20th goal.
11-24	@Florida	W	3-1		2nd	-3	Mark Recchi reached 1,500 career points.
11-26	Carolina	L	3-0		2nd	-3	Hurricanes went three-for-three on the power play.
11-28	@Atlanta	L	4-1		2nd	-5	Bruins fell to 0-5-2 when trailing after first period.
12-1	@Philadelphia	W	3-0		2nd	-4	Thomas stopped penalty shot, made 41 saves.
12-2	Tampa Bay	W	8-1		2nd	-4	Marc Savard returned, David Krejci scored twice in season's biggest rout.
12-4	@Toronto	O(SO)	2-2		2nd	-5	Former Bruin Phil Kessel netted winner in shootout.
12-7	Buffalo	W(OT)	3-2		2nd	-5	Recchi tipped in Dennis Seidenberg's slapshot in OT.
12-9	NY Islanders	W	5-2		2nd	-3	Milan Lucic scored two goals, Rask with 33 saves.
12-11	Philadelphia	O(OT)	2-1		2nd	-2	Mike Richards won it for Flyers with three seconds left in OT.
12-15	@Buffalo	L	3-2		2nd	-2	Buffalo's Drew Stafford collected hat trick.
12-16	@Montreal	L	4-3		2nd	-4	Canadiens kept Bruins in second place.
12-18	Washington	W	3-2		2nd	-2	Andrew Ference scored first goal in 100 games.
12-20	Anaheim	L	3-0		2nd	-2	Jonas Hiller denied Bruins with 45 saves.
12-23	Atlanta	W	4-1		2nd	-2	Shawn Thornton scored twice, game ended with melee.
12-27	@Florida	W(SO)	2-2		1st	T	Blake Wheeler's shootout goal put Bruins in first.
12-28	@Tampa Bay	W	4-3		1st	+2	Recchi tallied with 19.7 seconds remaining.
12-30	@Atlanta	O(SO)	2-2		1st	+3	Winning streak snapped at three.
1-1	@Buffalo	O(SO)	6-6		1st	+2	Stafford tied it with 28 seconds left, Sabres won in shootout.
1-3	@Toronto	W	2-1		1st	+3	Savard's winner capped 3-0-2 road trip.
1-6	Minnesota	L	3-1		1st	+1	Phantom hooking call on Thornton proved costly.
1-8	@Montreal	O(OT)	3-2		1st	T	Max Pacioretty's OT goal tied Canadiens for first.
1-10	@Pittsburgh	W	4-2		1st	+2	Four goals in final three and a half minutes shocked Penguins.

DATE	OPPONENT		SCORE	PLACE	UP/DOWN	NOTABLE
1-11	Ottawa	W	6-0	1st	+2	Patrice Bergeron netted first career hat trick.
1-13	Philadelphia	W	7-5	1st	+4	With five-goal third period, Bruins were 7-1-3 in last 11.
1-15	Pittsburgh	L	3-2	1st	+2	Seidenberg, Ryder scored 13 seconds apart to erase 2-0 deficit.
1-17	Carolina	W	7-0	1st	+2	Zdeno Chara had hat trick, Thomas posted seventh shutout.
1-18	@Carolina	W	3-2	1st	+3	A season-high 43 saves for Thomas.
1-20	Buffalo	L	4-2	1st	+3	Bruins lost for second time in 23 games when scoring first.
1-22	@Colorado	W	6-2	1st	+2	Lucic, Marchand each scored twice.
1-24	@Los Angeles	L	2-0	1st	+2	Kings snapped 0-for-22 power play drought.
1-26	Florida	W	2-1	1st	+4	Thomas headed to All-Star game with 1.81 goals-against-average.
2-1	@Carolina	W	3-2	1st	+4	Bergeron potted the game-winner.
2-3	Dallas	W	6-3	1st	+4	Three fights in first four seconds were prelude to victory.
2-5	San Jose	L	2-0	1st	+2	Sharks won despite just 18 shots.
2-9	Montreal	W	8-6	1st	+4	Even goalies Thomas and Price fought in penalty-filled brawl.
2-11	Detroit	L	6-1	1st	+3	Red Wings scored on first two shots.
2-13	@Detroit	L	4-2	1st	+1	Second-period shot advantage of 19-6 spurred Red Wings.
2-15	Toronto	L	4-3	1st	T	Bruins lost three straight for only time all season.
2-17	@NY Islanders	W	6-3	1st	+2	Rask stopped 34, six Bruins scored goals.
2-18	@Ottawa	W	4-2	1st	+4	Marchand's two goals highlighted three-goal third period.
2-22	@Calgary	W	3-1	1st	+4	Thomas back after week off, lowered goals-against to 1.99.
2-26	@Vancouver	W	3-1	1st	+4	Lucic netted winner in lone meeting between Cup finalists.
2-27	@Edmonton	W	3-2	1st	+6	Bruins posted 40-17 shot cushion.
3-1	@Ottawa	W	1-0	1st	+6	Rask earned shutout, Bruins completed 6-0 road trip.
3-3	Tampa Bay	W	2-1	1st	+6	Seventh straight win lifted B's to No. 2 in East.
3-5	Pittsburgh	O(OT)	3-2	1st	+5	Streak snapped on Dustin Jeffrey's OT goal.
3-8	@Montreal	L	4-1	1st	+3	Game marred by Chara's hit on Pacioretty.
3-10	Buffalo	O(OT)	4-3	1st	+4	Brad Boyes beat Bruins in overtime.
3-11	@NY Islanders	L	4-2	1st	+4	Islanders scored three in the third.
3-15	@Columbus	W(SO)	2-2	1st	+4	Seguin was only player to tally in shootout.
3-17	@Nashville	O(OT)	4-3	1st	+3	Shea Weber scored for Maple Leafs with 1:23 left.
3-19	@Toronto	L	5-2	1st	+3	Bruins 1-3-3 in last seven games.
3-22	New Jersey	W	4-1	1st	+3	Chara collected game-winner to stop slide.
3-24	Montreal	W	7-0	1st	+5	Gregory Campbell scored with B's at 5-on-3 disadvantage.
3-26	NY Rangers	L	1-0	1st	+5	Rangers goalie Henrik Lundqvist was unbeatable.
3-27	@Philadelphia	W	2-1	1st	+7	Marchand won it with 3:43 left.
3-29	Chicago	W	3-0	1st	+7	Recchi moved to 12th on all-time scoring list.
3-31	Toronto	O(SO)	3-3	1st	+8	Bruins clinched tie for Northeast Division title.
4-2	Atlanta	W	3-2	1st	+8	Ryder scored on penalty shot.
4-4	@NY Rangers	L	5-3	1st	+8	Rangers erased 3-0 deficit.
4-6	NY Islanders	W	3-2	1st	+8	Thornton scored as first period ended.
4-9	Ottawa	W	3-1	1st	+7	Thomas set save-percentage record at .938.
4-10	@New Jersey	L	3-2	1st	+7	Devils coach Jacques Lemaire retired with a win.